THE NATURE OF THE OUTER BANKS

THE UNIVERSITY OF NORTH CAROLINA PRESS   CHAPEL HILL AND LONDON

THE NATURE OF
THE OUTER BANKS

ENVIRONMENTAL PROCESSES, FIELD SITES,

AND DEVELOPMENT ISSUES, COROLLA TO OCRACOKE

Dirk Frankenberg

Illustrations by Linda Noble

Design by April Leidig-Higgins

The paper in this book meets the guidelines for permanence and durability of the Committee on Production Guidelines for Book Longevity of the Council on Library Resources.

99 98 97 96 95

5 4 3 2 1

Library of Congress Cataloging-in-Publication Data

Frankenberg, Dirk.

The nature of the Outer Banks : environmental processes, field sites, and development issues, Corolla to Ocracoke / by Dirk Frankenberg.

p. cm.

Includes bibliographical references and index.

ISBN 0-8078-4542-6 (pbk.: alk. paper)

1. Outer Banks (N.C.) — Environmental conditions. 2. Environmental sciences — North Carolina — Outer Banks. 3. Environmental policy — North Carolina — Outer Banks. I. Title.

GE155.N8F73 1995

508.756'1 — dc20   95-9913

CIP

This book is dedicated to two groups of people:

the students, alumni, and friends of the
University of North Carolina at Chapel Hill
who have visited the Outer Banks with me and
asked the good questions that sent me back
to libraries and field sites to gather information
for this book

the Outer Banks residents, environmentalists,
and public servants whose efforts have preserved
the natural areas that still allow us to observe
the nature of the Outer Banks

CONTENTS

FIGURES AND TABLES

Figures

Tables

PREFACE

This book grew out of my teaching at the University of North Carolina at Chapel Hill. My courses in oceanography and coastal processes always include field trips to allow students to see firsthand what they have heard about in lectures and read about in textbooks. Studying nature in the field is far more effective than learning about it from books—a fact pointed out in the mid-1800s by Louis Agassiz, a pioneer in marine biology who is widely quoted as saying, "Study nature, not books." I hope this book will encourage its readers to follow Agassiz's admonition and study nature directly.

The natural environment of the Outer Banks provides an excellent setting for the direct study of natural processes. It is the focus of this book for both specific and general reasons. First, most people visit the Banks to experience the environment; and second, the environment shapes the Banks' structure and appearance in ways that are relatively easy to observe and understand. The nature of the Outer Banks is a function of three major environmental processes: rising sea level, transport of sand by wind and water, and immobilization of sand by plant growth. Chapter 1 details how these three processes affect the environmental features of the Outer Banks. The interaction of these processes and the specific Outer Banks habitats produced by these interactions are described in Chapter 2, a mile-by-mile field guide to Outer Banks habitats between Corolla and Ocracoke. Finally, Chapter 3 examines human use of Outer Banks resources—fish, water, and land.

The Outer Banks cannot be fully understood without knowledge of the human impact on the environment. Outer Bankers today must face many development issues, three of which are discussed in Chapter 3: the status of fish stocks, freshwater supply, and wastewater disposal. This discussion illustrates the fact that natural resources are finite—a fact that is true everywhere but is particularly striking in the relatively simple and isolated environment of the Outer Banks.

An analysis of the human history of the Outer Banks reveals encouraging signs that their human inhabitants have come to realize that they cannot completely control the environment in which they live. For example, the National Park Service now observes a policy of not protecting human construction from damage by natural forces, and some Outer Banks towns have accepted the fact that oceanfront real estate may be lost in storms. These policies are an indication that modern society is learning to live with nature.

I hope that those who read this book will experience the beauty and fun of the Outer Banks firsthand. I also hope that those who come to know the Banks will realize that living with their nature is the best course for the future.

Many people helped make this book possible. I have dedicated it to students and friends whose questions helped me prepare to write it and to those who have labored to preserve natural areas on the Banks, many of whom I do not know personally. I am delighted that, largely because of the efforts of these preservationists, I could write a field guide rather than a history of what used to be.

Others who helped with the book include my wife Susan, our daughter Elizabeth, and our son Eben, who all read and constructively criticized early drafts — drafts that I wouldn't have shown to anyone except blood relatives. Susan, in particular, provided a masterful mix of encouragement and goading that helped bring the book to conclusion. My friend Watts Hill, Jr., took many of the photographs that illustrate the text and joined me in the fieldwork. Ries Collier of the National Park Service and B. J. Copeland and Lundie Spence of the University of North Carolina Sea Grant Program all read the manuscript in an early form, corrected errors, and identified sections that were difficult to comprehend. Sharon McBride typed the manuscript efficiently and with unflagging enthusiasm for the project. Linda Noble, the creative illustrator, deserves much credit for her illustrations. Finally, David Perry, Paula Wald, and their colleagues and reviewers at the University of North Carolina Press offered constructive advice that improved the manuscript. Any errors that remain are my own. Also, this book describes features of the Outer Banks that existed at the time of writing; since the Banks landscape is continually changing, some of these features may change over time. You can explore for yourself the changes that have occurred.

THE NATURE OF THE OUTER BANKS

CHAPTER ONE

ENVIRONMENTAL PROCESSES

The Outer Banks of North Carolina are unique among the world's coastal landforms in their distance from the mainland and their distinct shape. Scientists have labeled such offshore islands barrier islands because they serve as barriers between the wave and tidal energy of the ocean and the mainland shoreline. Barrier islands extend along the coast of the United States from Maine to Texas, but none are situated as far from the mainland as the Outer Banks and few have a shape that differs from that of the coast they parallel. The Outer Banks are 20 to 40 miles offshore and have a shape all their own. They have been shaped by the ocean into long, crescentic beaches stretching between four major capes. Such landforms, called cuspate forelands, usually form between rocky headlands, such as those along the coast of Brazil. The Outer Banks are unique in that their cuspate forelands have developed between the massive sandy shoals that extend seaward from each cape.

The Outer Banks region is an attractive place to live in or to visit. The separation of the islands from the mainland provides a sense of being "at sea." The islands' seasonal temperature range is narrower than that on the mainland because the surrounding waters absorb heat in the summer and give off heat in the winter. The waters themselves are ideal for swimming, boating, and fishing. Winds blow almost constantly to provide sport for sailors, hang-gliding enthusiasts, and kite flyers. Pleasant as the Banks may be, though, residents are always aware that destructive storms can spring up within hours. Reminders of this fact are everywhere, including the images of beachfront homes in the surf at Kitty Hawk, the roof of a Putt-Putt Golf Course jutting out of Jockey's Ridge, massive sandbags protecting NC 12, a stone jetty shielding the south side of Oregon Inlet from erosion, and steel walls, sandbags, and sand fences securing the beach in front of Cape Hatteras Lighthouse.

Inlet Dynamics, Sea Level Rise, and Landward Migration

The sea has flooded the Outer Banks many times. Those of us who live on stable landforms are surprised to learn just how flood-prone and unstable the Outer Banks have been. Inlets are probably the best example. Currently 5 inlets exist between Cape Lookout and the Virginia border. In the past, as many as 9 inlets have been open at once, and at least 24 have existed along this stretch of shoreline since colonial times. Figure 1 maps the location of known inlets between Virginia and Portsmouth Island since the 1500s.

Outer Banks inlets have opened and closed repeatedly during recorded history. When the first English-speaking colony was established on Roanoke Island in 1585, an inlet reportedly existed directly seaward of the island. It closed in the early 1800s. One of the colony's resupply vessels foundered in an inlet north of Cape Hatteras that subsequently closed in the 1650s, reopened in 1962, and was closed again during the construction of a highway. The inlet closure with the greatest environmental impact, however, occurred further north. Several inlets once connected the ocean

Figure 1. Historical and modern inlets of the Outer Banks. Seawater channels through the Outer Banks have occurred at many different places and times. Only three modern inlets exist along the Outer Banks — Oregon, Hatteras, and Ocracoke — but at least six existed in the 1840s. Data from David Stick, *The Outer Banks of North Carolina* (Chapel Hill: University of North Carolina Press, 1958), and J. J. Fisher, "Geomorphic Expression of Former Inlets along the Outer Banks of North Carolina" (master's thesis, University of North Carolina at Chapel Hill, 1962); base map from North Carolina Department of Transportation.

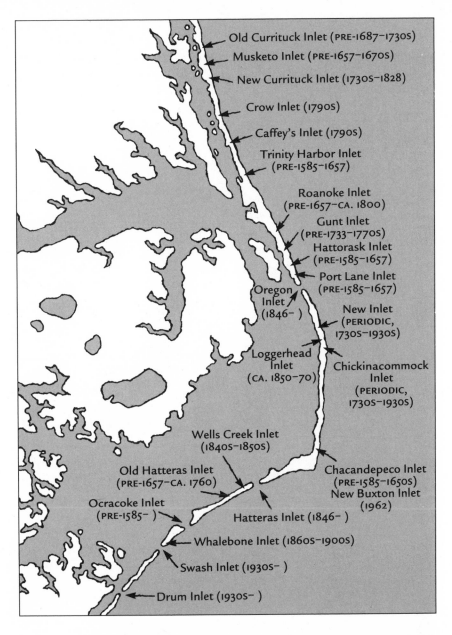

Old Currituck Inlet (PRE-1687–1730S)

Musketo Inlet (PRE-1657–1670S)

New Currituck Inlet (1730S–1828)

Crow Inlet (1790S)

Caffey's Inlet (1790S)

Trinity Harbor Inlet (PRE-1585–1657)

Roanoke Inlet (PRE-1657–CA. 1800)

Gunt Inlet (PRE-1733–1770S)

Hattorask Inlet (PRE-1585–1657)

Port Lane Inlet (PRE-1585–1657)

Oregon Inlet (1846–)

New Inlet (PERIODIC, 1730S–1930S)

Loggerhead Inlet (CA. 1850–70)

Chickinacommock Inlet (PERIODIC, 1730S–1930S)

Wells Creek Inlet (1840S–1850S)

Old Hatteras Inlet (PRE-1657–CA. 1760)

Chacandepeco Inlet (PRE-1585–1650S)

New Buxton Inlet (1962)

Ocracoke Inlet (PRE-1585–)

Hatteras Inlet (1846–)

Whalebone Inlet (1860S–1900S)

Swash Inlet (1930S–)

Drum Inlet (1930S–)

to the 40-mile-long lagoon made up of Currituck Sound in North Carolina and Back Bay in Virginia. The last of these inlets, New Currituck, was closed by natural sedimentation in 1828. Within 50 years, over 100 square miles of brackish water and salt marsh were converted to freshwater lagoon and marsh. This change was termed "one of the most important geological changes which has taken place along the Atlantic coast in recent times" by G. R. Weiland, who described the effect of the inlet closing in the *American Journal of Science* in 1897.

The constant movement of sand and water alters the shape of inlets every day, but the most striking change occurs when inlets open. The process begins when large storms push water through and over the Banks and into the sounds behind them. Surprisingly, this landward movement of water rarely opens permanent inlets. New inlets are formed by the subsequent seaward flow when winds rotating counterclockwise around the storm center blow water back toward the ocean. The force of this flow, especially when focused on an area weakened by preceding flooding, moves enough sand to form a new inlet (see figure 2). The hurricane of 1846 was the champion of recent inlet-opening storms. Both Oregon and Hatteras inlets opened after it traveled up the coast.

Inlets close when more sand is brought into them than can be removed by tidal currents flowing through them. Inlet closure is usually a slow process. Small additions of sand accumulate in the tidal channels, thereby decreasing their size. The smaller channels carry less water, which in turn clears less sand from the channels. Eventually, beaches and dunes form across what was once the mouth of the inlet. We can see this happening today in Ocracoke Inlet. Once the major shipping route through the Banks, it now provides navigable channels best suited for relatively small vessels.

Inlet formation may be the most dramatic erosional process along the Outer Banks, but it is by no means the only one. The balance between erosion and deposition of sand affects practically every feature of Banks geography. As a result, the geography of the Outer Banks is in a constant state of change. Beaches erode and accrete as sand is removed or added; sandbars form and disappear; navigation channels shift; islands change shape as terminal sand spits elongate; dunes form, disappear, and migrate

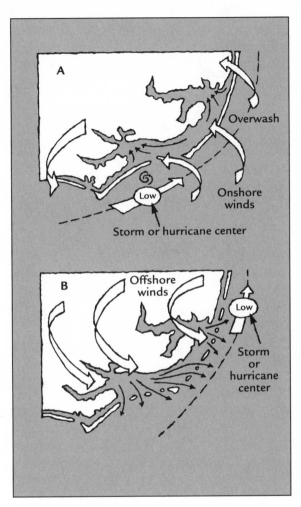

Figure 2. Inlet formation. Inlets form when storms drive water across the Outer Banks. (A) As storms and hurricanes approach from the south, onshore winds cause seawater to wash over the Banks and into the sounds. (B) After the storm has moved northeastward, offshore winds and gravity drive water back toward the ocean, sometimes washing away so much sand that new inlets are formed. Both Oregon and Hatteras inlets opened as a result of flooding from the sounds during the hurricane of 1846. Redrawn from Stephen P. Leatherman, *Barrier Island Handbook*, Coastal Publications Series (College Park: University of Maryland Press, 1988), fig. 39, p. 39.

to places they have never been before. Anyone familiar with the Banks knows that these events are not unusual; in fact, the only constant in natural Banks habitats is that they are constantly changing.

Some changes follow seasonal cycles in prevailing winds and alter the Banks in one way part of the time and the opposite way at other times. Other changes continue in one direction for long periods. Rising sea level plays a part in many Banks processes, including beach erosion, the movement of sand to the landward side of islands during overwash events, and the deposition of sand in inlets. Geologists Douglas Inman and Robert Dolan have studied these processes as well as old maps and aerial photographs of the Banks and have concluded that the beachface of the Outer Banks north of Cape Hatteras is moving closer to the mainland at a rate of almost 5 feet per year. This movement is called landward retreat or shoreface recession and is mostly caused by rising sea level: directly, when the ocean occupies areas that once were beach; and indirectly, through processes that remove sand from the shoreface. Inman and Dolan estimate that 21 percent of shoreface recession on the Outer Banks is a direct result of rising sea level. They maintain that 65 percent is indirectly caused by rising sea level: 31 percent, when waves wash sand over the dunes and into the interior or sound side of the island; 17 percent, when sand is deposited along offshore bars and shoals; and another 17 percent, when sand accumulates in inlets. The final 14 percent is blown off the beach and into the island interior by onshore winds.

Barrier islands such as the Outer Banks are shoreline features — they form wherever the sea surface stays in contact with sedimentary coastal material for an extended period of time. Since sea level has been rising for the last 17,000 years, most barrier islands have moved landward to a point quite close to the mainland. The Outer Banks have not. The reason for their unusually great distance from the mainland remains a mystery.

Sea level was about 300 feet lower than it is now 17,000 years ago. At that time, glacial ice sheets covered Canada and the northern United States as far south as Wisconsin, Michigan, New York, and Massachusetts. As the climate warmed, the glaciers melted, the ocean warmed, and sea level rose to its present position. Fossil evidence indicates that it did not rise at a constant rate. As shown in figure 3, the rise was rapid (about

1 inch per decade) from 12,500 to 4,000 years ago but slowed to about ⅛ that rate thereafter. This general pattern seems to have occurred in North Carolina, as recent tide gauge records show a current rate of rise of about ⅐ inch per decade along the Outer Banks. At some point during this last period of rising sea level, barrier islands formed at the shoreface and began migrating landward. Coastal geologists do not agree when barrier islands similar to the present Outer Banks may have formed. Some think they formed when the rate of sea level rise slowed.

Sea level has also been as much as 300 feet higher than it is now. At that time (85 million years ago), the coastline and its barrier islands were located near Fayetteville, Goldsboro, Wilson, and Rocky Mount, about where Interstate 95 now lies. One hundred and twenty-five thousand years ago, the ocean shoreline extended from Swansboro through Aurora, Bath, and Plymouth to Suffolk, Virginia, along the sandy ridge upon which parts of NC 306, 32, and 45 have been built.

Sand Transport by Wind and Water

The environmental processes that move the Outer Banks landward during periods of rising sea level begin on the beaches. To understand them, we must therefore examine the beaches themselves (hard work, but someone has to do it). The easiest process to observe is wind transport of sand. Whenever the wind is blowing briskly — the norm on the Outer Banks — it transports fine sand up the beach. This sand is usually deposited in the dunes landward of the beach because the strongest winds blow from the ocean toward the land. Within the dunes, sand continues to move. Dunes grow taller or migrate as sand is blown up the windward face and deposited on the leeward face. A steep, soft face on the downwind side is a sure indication of an actively moving dune. Some very large migrating dunes can be seen on the Outer Banks. Jockey's Ridge in Nags Head is the best known example, but at least ten dunes of similar size have existed in the recent past between Nags Head and the Virginia border. Here the Banks run southeast to northwest, an orientation at right angles to the two directions from which winds most often blow — southwest and

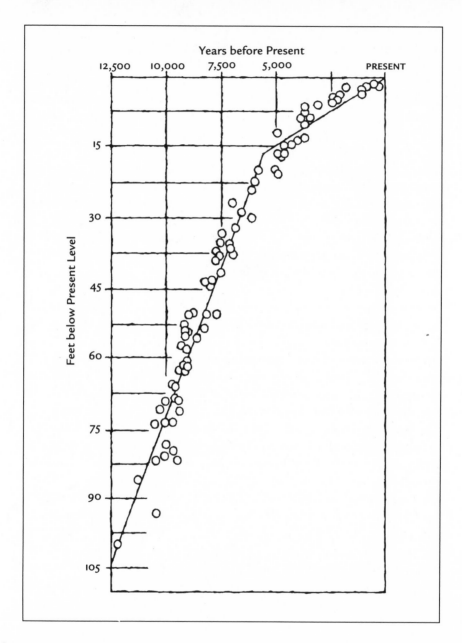

northeast. Figure 4 shows the wind direction frequencies in the Outer Banks averaged over a year, in the winter, and in the summer, as recorded at Cape Hatteras by the U.S. Weather Service from 1965 through 1978.

North of Nags Head, northeast winds blow sand off the beach and up the dune face and deposit it southwest of the dune crest. Later, southwest winds pick up the same sand and carry it over the crest to settle on the northeast face. Back and forth the sand shifts, some of it remaining behind each time, thus making the dune taller. Eventually, giant dunes are formed; these dunes may migrate somewhat, but they persist for long periods of time, many having served as useful navigational landmarks throughout Banks history. Figure 5 shows where the major giant dunes of the Outer Banks are located and diagrams the environmental process whereby alternating winds form and maintain such dunes.

Less visible than wind transport of sand, but quantitatively more important to the overall landward retreat of the Outer Banks, is the transport of sand by breaking waves and coastal currents. Waves are created on the sea surface when some force disturbs that surface. The most common waves are caused by wind, but other types of waves exist: submarine earthquakes cause large waves called tsunamis; tides are caused by the inequality between gravitation and centripetal forces between the earth, moon, and sun; and differences in atmospheric pressure around storms cause storm surges. These various types of waves differ from one another in length, speed, and frequency.

Common wind waves are important sand movers on the Outer Banks. Wind blowing across the ocean creates waves that bring energy to the shore. As waves approach the beach, friction from the interaction with the seafloor slows their forward progress, causing them to shorten and steepen. When the height-to-length ratio exceeds 1 to 7, waves break and

Figure 3. Change in sea level, 12,500 years ago to the present. Data for this figure was collected in Bermuda, an island far removed from continents, earthquakes, and volcanoes, thus as likely as anyplace to have had a sea level history like that of the earth as a whole. Sea level change on the Outer Banks has been more rapid than that recorded in this figure. Modified from Dieter Meishner and A. Conrad Neumann, "Holocene Sea Level Rise, Bermuda" (unpublished manuscript, 1994).

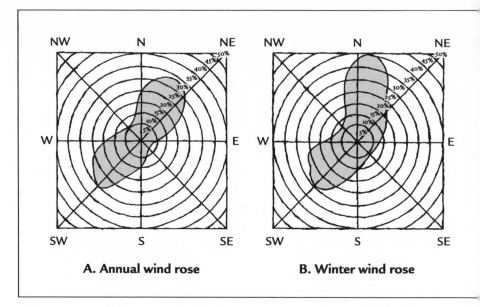

Figure 4. Windfields at Cape Hatteras. These graphs plot the percentage of winds that come from each direction of the compass. The annual pattern (A) shows that winds come from the northeast and southwest more than from any other direction. This is called a bimodal windfield. Note that in winter (B), winds come more

release their stored energy in the surf zone. As breakers roll through the surf zone, they move sand grains, thus beginning the processes of sand transport, beach erosion, and beach accretion.

Not all waves break in the same way (see figure 6). Spend some time watching breakers, and you will see the difference. In some waves, the wave crest is thrown forward and plunges down the wave front, creating a curl of water that traps a "tube" of air in front of the breaker. Scientists, literal-minded souls that they are, call these plunging breakers. Other waves break less dramatically, the crest simply spilling down the front of the wave in a froth of water and air bubbles. These are called spilling breakers. Both plunging and spilling breakers erode sand from the beach.

Spilling and plunging breakers are easier to identify than collapsing

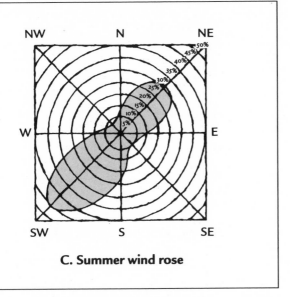

NW   N   NE

50%
45%
40%
35%
30%
25%
20%
15%
10%
5%

W   E

SW   S   SE

C. Summer wind rose

from the north, while in summer (C), southwest winds are more common than any other type. Data on monthly wind direction at Cape Hatteras, 1965–78, from U.S. Weather Service.

breakers. Collapsing breakers occur on short, steep waves approaching relatively steeply sloped beaches. As the wave nears the shore, the bottom half of the face collapses forward, removing support for the wave crest, which collapses downward, forcing a surge of water up onto the beach. This surge moves sand onto the beach rather than off the beach. Most breakers spill or plunge; only on special days and in special places are collapsing breakers common, but careful observers can see some collapsing breakers even among the multitude of those that plunge and spill. A student of mine once wrote in a field trip report: "The Professor said that he saw collapsing breakers, but none of the students saw them, and they are much younger than he is." The frustration is understandable because collapsing breakers are indeed difficult to distinguish, but time spent watch-

Figure 5. Winds and giant dunes on the northern Outer Banks. The bimodal windfield of the Outer Banks creates giant dunes (such as Jockey's Ridge and Run Hill) by blowing sand to the dune crest from the northeast and southwest. This figure shows the location of giant dunes and the prevailing winds blowing directly onshore or offshore (A) and illustrates how sand is carried to the dune crest by winds from the northeast (B) and the southwest (C).

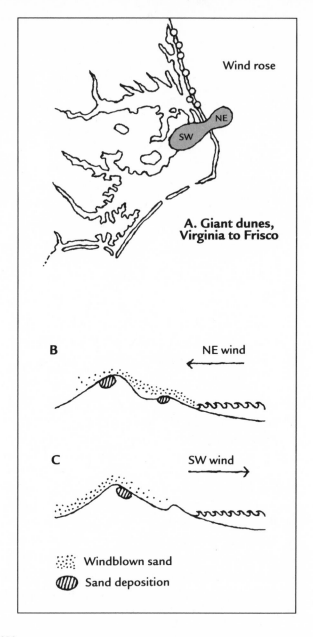

Wind rose

NE

SW

A. Giant dunes, Virginia to Frisco

B

NE wind

C

SW wind

Windblown sand

Sand deposition

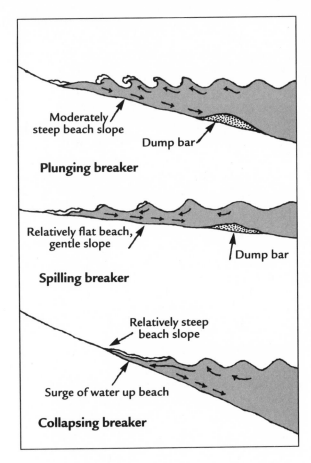

Figure 6. Types of breakers: plunging, spilling, and collapsing. Plunging and spilling breakers move sand off the beach; water moves landward at the top of the breaker and seaward along the submerged beachface, carrying sand offshore. Collapsing breakers move sand up the beach toward land; the collapse of the wave face causes a surge of water up the beach that has more power to move sand than does its backwash.

Labels within figure:
- Moderately steep beach slope
- Dump bar
- **Plunging breaker**
- Relatively flat beach, gentle slope
- Dump bar
- **Spilling breaker**
- Relatively steep beach slope
- Surge of water up beach
- **Collapsing breaker**

ing breakers is never time wasted—the plot may be dull, but a sighting of the rare collapsing breaker provides a unique conversational opening for meeting other beachgoers.

The different mechanics of the various types of breakers can be easily discerned by anyone swimming or standing in the surf zone. If you are surrounded by plunging and spilling breakers, you will feel water rushing past your upper body as the breaker moves landward and then undermining the sand from beneath your feet as the wave recedes. In other words, the water in the broken part of the wave moves toward shore, along the surface of the ocean, sometimes even while backwash from the previous breaker moves seaward along the seafloor. This two-layer flow pattern in the wave — landward in the broken wave crest on top and seaward in the backwash along the bottom — means that the water in direct contact with the beach sediment is moving seaward. Any sand transported by such water is removed from the beach, resulting in beach erosion. A collapsing breaker is quite different: the water in contact with the sand during the break moves landward. The breaking wave moves landward until it reaches its maximum height on the beach, then all the water moves back toward the sea. The movement up the beach is powered by the energy of the wave collapse, but the subsequent backwash is not; therefore, the landward surge is more powerful. That surge picks up sand and carries it up the beach; the less powerful backwash, which is also slowed down by friction with the seafloor, does not carry the sand as far back toward the sea. Sand moved by collapsing breakers accumulates on the beach, causing the beach to grow or "accrete."

By identifying types of breakers, you can determine whether the beach is losing or gaining sand while you are looking at it. Spilling breakers are usually visible somewhat offshore. To locate them, watch for crests that spill foam down the front of the wave. Look for plunging breakers close to the beach. The final act of most waves that reach the Outer Banks is to plunge onto the beach. Plunging breakers are characterized by a curl of water springing out of the wave crest and plunging down over the wave face, as in televised images of surf in Hawaii and California. Finally, collapsing breakers occur where the ocean meets the beach. Typical collapsing breakers steepen to an almost triangular cross section before they break. Look for impossibly steep wave faces that shoot water forward from the bottom rather than from the top, as in spilling and plunging breakers.

The movement of sand by breakers drives the patterns of beach erosion and accretion that dominate Outer Banks geography. The beaches are literally moving. Not only does sand move onshore and offshore, but it also moves along the shore whenever waves break at an angle to the shoreface, which is most of the time. As a result, beaches are constantly shifting, and their future position can be predicted only as well as we can predict the size and direction of the waves that break upon them — in other words, not very well. However, we can make three predictions. First, beach sands will move; second, beach erosion will be more common than beach accretion when sea level is rising; and third, sand will be transported along the shore in a direction controlled in the long term (weeks to years) by prevailing winds and in the short term (hours to weeks) by the wind and waves occurring at the time.

Huge amounts of sand may be moved along the shore. Inman and Dolan estimate that 500,000 to 1 million cubic yards of sand are transported along the Outer Banks each year. Considering that a large dump truck carries only 15 cubic yards per load, annual sand transport along the Banks moves the equivalent of about 66,000 dump truck loads. In economic terms, based on a cost of about $8 per cubic yard of sand, the amount of sand involved in natural sand movement each year would cost about $8 million, but as you can imagine, it doesn't always end up where you want it.

More sand is moved onshore and offshore than is moved along the shore. This onshore-offshore transport is part of a "sand-sharing system" that operates between the oceanfront dune and the offshore sandbars. Sand eroded from the beach or dune by plunging or spilling breakers is moved offshore to depths so great that it can no longer be transported by the prevailing waves. Beyond this depth (the wave base), the sand settles to the bottom and becomes part of an offshore bar. Later, when the sandbar begins to extend above the wave base and collapsing waves return, the sands of the offshore bar are resuspended and moved back onto the beach. This movement onto the beach occurs so slowly and under such calm conditions that it can only be seen clearly by using time-lapse photography. Beachgoers can discover evidence of the process, however, by watching for sandbars that appear stranded on the beach. Usually these bars create long, narrow tidepools on their landward side. Repeated visits to the same location will show that the stranded bar moves up the beach until it disappears as its sand is incorporated into the beachface.

The beachfront sand-sharing system operates continuously, but during storms it broadens to include more offshore bars and the coastal dunefield. Storm waves move sand over amazingly large areas. The bigger the wave, the further seaward its influence is felt. Large offshore bars exist along the continental shelf off the Outer Banks; these bars or "sand waves" remain stationary for long periods of time and move only in the largest storms. Coastal dunefields may also be stable for a long time before being eroded away during a storm. Figure 7 illustrates both the "normal" sand-sharing system and its extension during storm conditions.

The sand-sharing system seems quite benign, but, much like toy-sharing systems designed by adults for use by children, sometimes one component of the system holds onto things longer than other components can tolerate. Figure 7 illustrates one sand-holding component of the system. Overwash deposits or fans are formed when sand washes over the dunes and settles on the island or in the sound behind it. Overwash processes remove more sand from Outer Banks beaches than any other process and account for 39 percent of the Banks' landward retreat. They occur when high tides and high waves exist at the same time, most frequently in fall, winter, and spring but sometimes in summer storms as well. Hurricanes and northeasters cause overwashes all along the Outer Banks.

Two other major sand-holding areas along the Banks are inlets and offshore shoals. These areas receive sand from the beaches after it is picked up by waves and carried into coastal currents, which move parallel to the shore. Along the Outer Banks, these currents generally flow southward from Virginia to Cape Hatteras and westward from Frisco to Ocracoke. When sand being moved along the shore comes to the end of an island or a sharp bend in the shoreface, it settles out, forming a deposit on the seafloor. At the end of an island, it enters the inlet, where it creates ebb- and flood-tide deltas. These deltas shift constantly, making inlet channels treacherous to navigate. Sand and water are always traveling through inlets. Inlets open, inlets close, inlets become deeper or shallower, inlets migrate from place to place. Inlets are dynamic because of the sand carried into, through, and around them. Oregon Inlet stores 17 percent of the sand lost from northern Outer Banks beaches, and half of that is removed each year by dredging. When the Outer Banks make their unique right-angle turns from running north-south to running east-west, sand carried by alongshore currents continues southward to form the notorious

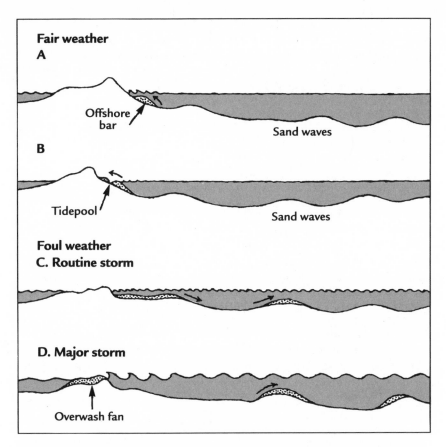

Fair weather
A

Offshore bar

Sand waves

B

Tidepool

Sand waves

Foul weather
C. Routine storm

D. Major storm

Overwash fan

Figure 7. The coastal sand-sharing system, fair weather and foul. In fair weather, collapsing breakers and tides move sand onto the beach from offshore bars (A), sometimes creating a narrow tidepool on the beach (B). In foul weather, spilling and plunging breakers erode sand from the beach and carry it offshore to form sandbars (C). In major storms, high waves and tides move sand over and between sand dunes to form overwash fans behind the dunes (D). Overwash events often carry sand onto roads and buildings built close to the beach.

shoals off the Carolina capes—Diamond Shoals off Cape Hatteras (see figure 8), Lookout Shoals off Cape Lookout, and Frying Pan Shoals off Cape Fear. These shoals stretch seaward more than 15 miles. Together, inlets and shoals account for most of the shipwrecks that have given the ocean off the Outer Banks the fearsome nickname "Graveyard of the Atlantic." Of the 445 vessels lost at sea off the Carolina capes between 1841 and 1930, 182 (41 percent) sank on or near offshore shoals and another 111 (25 percent) sank while trying to navigate inlets.

Shipwrecks occur in inlets and on shoals because sand deposits make these areas shallower than the surrounding sea. It is clear why ships must risk encountering inlet shallows as they come to port after "crossing the bar" of tidal deltas. It is less clear why ships go aground on offshore shoals. It helps to remember that almost all the ships that have wrecked off the North Carolina coast have been sailing vessels. Such ships had a hard time rounding the Carolina capes because they often met southwest winds when they were heading south or northeast winds when they were heading north. These adverse winds could hold a sailing ship on the downwind side of the capes for days. Over 100 ships often congregated near Cape Hatteras because their captains were unwilling to sail against the strong current near the Gulf Stream but also found it impossible to anchor. Such ships were forced to sail back and forth near the shoals while waiting for conditions to change. A minor mistake put them aground on the shoals, where heavy waves (especially at Cape Hatteras) pounded the vessels until they fell apart. These conditions and their consequences for seafarers are described more fully in Chapter 3.

Problems in navigating around shoals and through inlets are caused not only by the fact that sand is deposited in these areas but also by the fact that sand is always shifting around within them. The sand moves in response to tidal currents, alongshore transport of sand and water, and wave activity. These forces are hard to predict, making the specific location of natural navigation channels through inlets and around shoals difficult to estimate. The good news is that the general processes that form and move these seafloor features are reasonably well understood; the bad news is that this knowledge is very small consolation to any boat operator aground on a regrettably "specific" sandbar.

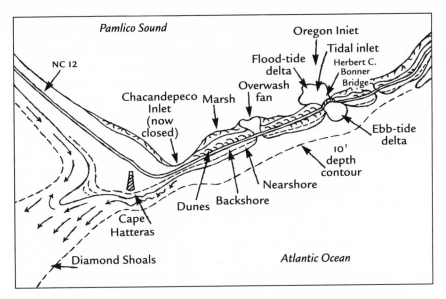

Figure 8. Alongshore transport and shoals. Waves, tides, and coastal currents move sand along the shore. Sand moving along the shore of the Outer Banks moves offshore at the capes to form shallow shoals stretching 10 to 15 miles seaward. Sand moving through inlets on tidal currents settles to form tidal deltas. Offshore shoals and tidal deltas are hazards to navigators. Together, these features account for most of the shipwrecks that have occurred near the Outer Banks.

The navigation problems in inlets are a result of tidal exchange of water between ocean and sound. Rising (flooding) tides carry water through the inlets to the sounds, and falling (ebbing) tides carry water back again seaward. When the water moves through the inlet, its velocity increases to reach a maximum at the narrowest part (the throat). Tidal currents at this point are strong enough to erode the seafloor. Inlet depths of 30 feet are common in North Carolina. Needless to say, few vessels go aground in the throats of inlets. The problems occur landward and seaward of the throat. Here the water spreads out as it reaches the sound or the ocean, causing the velocity of the flow to decrease. As a result, sand held in suspension in the rapid flow of the throat settles, forming sandbars and shifting chan-

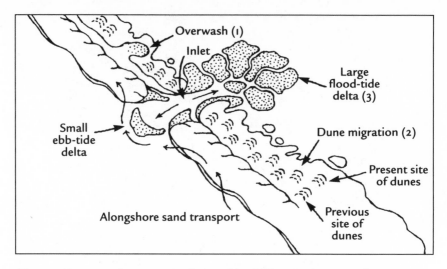

Figure 9. Processes that move sand toward land. Three environmental processes move sand toward land: (1) overwash events carry sand from the beach to behind the dunes; (2) onshore winds carry sand over dunes, causing them to migrate landward; and (3) flood tides carry sand to deltas on the landward side of inlets. Redrawn from Stephen P. Leatherman, *Barrier Island Handbook*, Coastal Publications Series (College Park: University of Maryland Press, 1988), fig. 49, p. 49.

nels. These bars and channels combine to form a sand body called a tidal delta because of its general similarity to the large deltas that form at the mouths of rivers (such as in the Nile, Indus, and Mississippi rivers). The tidal delta caused by flooding tides usually contains more sediment and has somewhat less rapidly shifting channels than that formed by ebbing tides. Flood-tide deltas store sand that is incorporated into the landward side of the island if the inlet closes. Ebb-tide deltas form seaward of the inlet and are especially dynamic and therefore hazardous to navigation because of their exposure to ocean waves.

Offshore waves shift sand and channels and, in combination with alongshore transport, move sand along the delta from the upstream to the downstream island. Scientists call this sand movement an inlet bypass system (see figures 9 and 10). These systems are important to main-

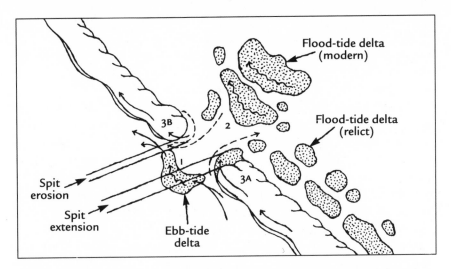

Figure 10. Sand transport across inlets. Sand moving alongshore can be carried to the downstream side of an inlet by 3 processes: (1) it can be carried to the ebb-tide delta and be moved across the inlet mouth by alongshore current, waves, and tidal currents; (2) it can be carried through the inlet to the flood-tide delta and be moved to the downstream side by waves and currents; or (3) it can activate the inlet by being deposited on the upstream sand spit (3a), thereby focusing tidal currents on the downstream side of the inlet, where they erode sand (3b) and carry it to downstream beaches. Modified from D. L. Inman and R. Dolan, "The Outer Banks of North Carolina: Budget of Sediment and Inlet Dynamics along a Migrating Barrier Island System," *Journal of Coastal Research* 5, no. 2 (1989): 219.

taining barrier islands because they transport sand from one side of the inlet to the other, thereby maintaining the sand supply to downstream island beaches. The importance of natural inlet bypass systems to the maintenance and survival of downstream lands requires that those who design systems to "stabilize" dynamic inlets must incorporate into their plans features that attempt to imitate natural systems. If they do not, they will face the continuing expense of dredging sand from places where it is not wanted (navigation channels) and moving it to places where it is urgently needed (beaches downstream from the inlet). Few inlet stabilization plans along any coast have provided effective substitutes for the natural inlet bypass system, and none have succeeded in inlets with the annual volume of sand transport that occurs on the Outer Banks.

Natural processes of island overwash and flood-tide delta formation move sand from the seaward side of barrier islands to the landward side. Much of the sand on today's Outer Banks was brought there as an overwash or flood-tide delta deposit. Such transfers are essential if the islands are to continue their landward retreat due to rising sea level. One other process, dune migration, also transports sand landward (see figure 11). This process can be observed whenever winds greater than about 25 mph are blowing. Strong winds pick up and carry along very fine sand grains. Beaches and dunes look "fuzzy" on top when these conditions occur. The "fuzz" is actually a 4- to 8-inch-thick layer of fine sand being carried by the wind. Since the strongest winds on the Outer Banks blow from the northeast, most dunes move to the south and west, that is, landward.

Sand Stabilization by Plants

Both visitors and residents of the Outer Banks have two reasons to display the bumper sticker that asks, "Have you thanked a green plant today?" Besides providing the food and oxygen that allow us to survive on earth, plants stabilize the landforms Outer Bankers inhabit. The enormous amount of sand that wind, waves, and currents set in motion is stopped and held in place by plants. Obviously the ability of plants to stabilize shifting sands has limits; the bare, unvegetated sand in overwash deposits, active dune faces, and elongating sand spits is evidence of those limits. But by and large, most Outer Banks sands are now covered with stabilizing vegetation.

The current degree of vegetation on the Banks is greater than it was earlier in this century and probably less than it was at the first European contact, when Captain Arthur Barlowe rhapsodized about the "goodly woods full of deere, hares and fowl in incredible abundance." The variation in Outer Banks vegetation levels over time is partially the work of humans. There is no doubt that overgrazing by cattle, sheep, goats, and horses contributed to an unusually bare sand environment along the Banks in the early twentieth century, a condition from which they are still recovering. Natural processes also create small areas of bare sand—dunes are over-washed and "blown out," dune migration leaves bare sand behind, inlet processes deposit bare sand on the shore. These bare sands gradually become vegetated. Vegetation develops in a sequence of stages, each one of which prepares for the next. These stages can easily be observed as one walks from the ocean to the sound. The first plants one encounters are sea oats and beach grass, which interrupt the smooth flow of wind along the beach and cause sand being transported to be deposited among them. In this way, they operate like a natural sand fence.

Behind the first (primary) dune, sea oats, beach grass, and other dune plants create a prairie that covers the sand with low vegetation. These plants are well adapted to the direct sunlight, high soil temperatures, and porous soils that occur in the dunes. The plants hold the sand in place with both above-ground and below-ground structures (see figure 12). Above the ground, the upright stems create a zone gentle winds cannot penetrate; as winds increase, the stems bend parallel to the sand surface, further protecting it from the direct effect of the winds. Below-ground structures become involved in sand stabilization when winds expose the extensive network of roots and rhizomes to produce an almost continuous blanket of plant matter over the sand (see figure 13). Sometimes, of course, storm winds and waves overwhelm the natural protection that plants provide. Dunes may "blow out" and migrate; primary dunes may become "cliffed" as waves wash sand out from under the plant cover; overwashed sand may cover plants, creating a new, bare sand surface. Nevertheless, plants provide the only natural protection for Outer Banks sands. Disturbing these plants is an invitation to dune migration problems.

A migrating dune is like an 800-pound gorilla: it goes wherever it wants. Outer Banks dunes have migrated over roads, gardens, houses, and whole communities. Sand from bare areas can travel long distances in an aperiodic move-and-settle pattern called saltation, but eventually it stops when it reaches either an obstruction or the crest of a dune. Visitors to the Banks can see recently deposited sand behind natural vegetation, on top of man-made objects, and on dune crests.

Figure II. Windblown
sand goes wherever it
wants. Wind carries
sand landward into
dunes, yards, and bath-
houses. Photographs
by Watts Hill, Jr.

The shape and morphology of dunes are related to the extent of vegetation growing on them (see figure 14). Linear dunes are heavily covered with vegetation. Dunes with lower percentages of vegetated areas are less regular and more hummocky. Blowouts and dune migration occur when dunes have little vegetative cover.

The establishment of dune plants is the first vegetated stage in a continuum that culminates in a full-fledged maritime forest. Protected areas within and downwind from the dunes contain shrubs, thickets, trees, and forests. The plant life that grows in island interiors is determined by wind speed, salt spray exposure, the amount of organic matter in the soil, and the constancy of the water supply. Different combinations of these environmental factors create prairies, thickets, and maritime forests. The plants that live in these different communities alter environmental processes by their very existence (see figures 15, 16, and 17). As a result, conditions constantly change to alter the chances of survival of plants characteristic of later stages of the sand stabilization sequence. Some dune plants, sea oats (*Uniola paniculata*), for example, tolerate salt spray expo-

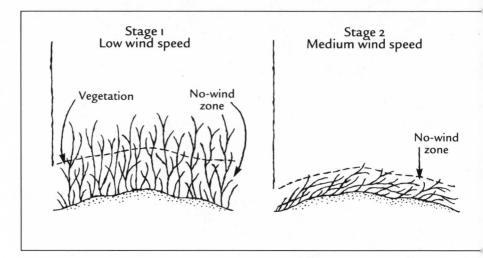

Figure 12. Dune plants trap and hold sand. Dune plants disrupt the windfield by creating turbulence. This results in a zone of no wind within the plant zone (stage 1). Sand blown into this no-wind zone will settle there. As winds increase, plants respond in ways that hold the settled sand in place. First, the plants are

sure better than others, such as salt meadow cordgrass (*Spartina patens*) or dune broom sedge (*Andropogon littoralis*). Consequently, plants such as cordgrass and broom sedge grow only in areas protected from salt spray by dense stands of sea oats or by frontal dunes.

Thicket and forest communities grow only in protected areas of the dunefield. The harmful effects of salt spray often keep these plants from extending very far above the top of the dune behind which they grow. Further back from the ocean, where wind speed and the amount of salt spray have been reduced by the wind's passage over dunes and sea oats, thicket plants like red cedar (*Juniperus virginiana*), groundsel (*Baccharis halimifolia*), marsh elder (*Iva frutescens*), and yaupon holly (*Ilex vomitoria*) can grow successfully. Thickets (sometimes called shrublands) can become so dense that it is hard to make your way through them. If you do enter a thicket, you can observe just how well these plant communities shield the sand from the effects of wind and salt spray. A layer of leaves protects the

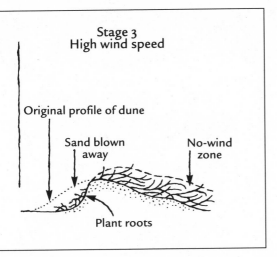

Stage 3
High wind speed

Original profile of dune

Sand blown
away

No-wind
zone

Plant roots

blown flat against the sand, thereby protecting as much sand as
possible from the erosive effect of the wind (stage 2). In the event
that sand is blown from beneath the plants, the roots of the plants
are exposed to further protect the sand that remains (stage 3).

ground's surface, and if you were to dig a hole, you would see that the
products of the decay of the leaf layer have worked their way down into
the sand to create layers of dark brown and yellow soil above the original
layer of white sand.

The impact of wind-driven salt spray alters the shape of individual
thicket plants and the canopies they combine to form (see figure 18). Individual plants are shaped when salt-laden winds stunt the branches on
the windward side, whereas on the leeward side, branches develop nor-
mally. The net effect of this differential growth is that the plants look
something like flags, with the trunk on the upwind side and most of the
branches and foliage on the downwind side. Cedars, live oaks, and thicket shrubs best illustrate this phenomenon, predictably called flagging by
botanists. Salt spray exposure determines the shape of thicket canopies
by encouraging ground-hugging growth on the windward side and increasingly taller growth further downwind. The windward plants absorb

Figure 13. Plants trap and stabilize windblown sand. Dune vegetation uprooted by erosion helps stabilize the dune from further erosion. Note root, rhizome, and plant material covering the eroded dune face. Photographs by author.

the brunt of salt spray exposure, thereby stunting their own growth but protecting the plants behind them. The resulting shape of the thicket is described as wedged. The top of the canopy is also shaped by salt spray, as twigs growing upward above the canopy in summer are killed back by salt spray during winter storms. The almost impenetrable network of branches at the top of the canopy keeps the salt-laden air from penetrating the interior. As a result, the sand under thickets is relatively undisturbed and develops organic-rich layers. Soil development sustains increasingly complex plant communities as moisture, nutrients, and organic matter increase and exposure to salt spray and blown sand decreases.

Landward of thickets are maritime forests. The patches of natural forest along the Outer Banks that remain undeveloped share many dominant species — such as slash pine, loblolly pine, and live oaks — but differ

from each other in their diversity, age, and subdominant species. The most fully developed maritime forest on the Outer Banks is Nags Head Woods. This forest has existed much longer than any other on the Outer Banks. Some estimate that it dates back to the onset of the Würm glaciation over 50,000 years ago. The plants and animals in the forest are remarkably diverse — so diverse, in fact, that Nags Head Woods is more like a piedmont or upper coastal plain forest than any other maritime forest on the Outer Banks. It contains over 300 species of plants, 100 species of birds, and 65 land vertebrates. Among the 46 species of reptiles and amphibians, 61 percent are usually found on the mainland, whereas only 39 percent are usually found on barrier islands. The maritime forest at Buxton Woods, by contrast, has existed for no more than about 6,000 years. Its reptiles and amphibians are less diverse (26 species), and barrier island species (65 percent) outnumber mainland species (35 percent). An even less mature maritime forest on the Outer Banks is located on Ocracoke at the site of the Hammock Hills Nature Trail. The forest is relatively young

A

B

Figure 14. Plant cover controls dune morphology. Dune features and morphology are related to the percentage of plant cover. (A) Full cover (more than 90%) maintains stable beach ridges; (B) less cover (75–90%) allows blowouts, producing discontinuous dunes; (C) moderate cover (45–75%) results in hummocky dunes; (D) less than 20% cover leads to unstable migrating dunes. Photograph A by Watts Hill, Jr.; B, C, and D by author.

C

D

Figure 15. Ecological conditions in dune-fields. Wind strength, salt spray exposure, soil moisture and nutrients, dune blowout frequency, and plant cover all differ at different points in a dunefield. This figure illustrates a cross section of an Outer Banks dunefield showing the shape of the primary, secondary, and tertiary dunes, the types of plants that grow near them, the depth of the water table, and the direction in which freshwater flows after reaching the dune as rainfall. It also shows the relative level of soil nutrients, soil moisture, and dune blowout frequency at different points in such a dunefield.

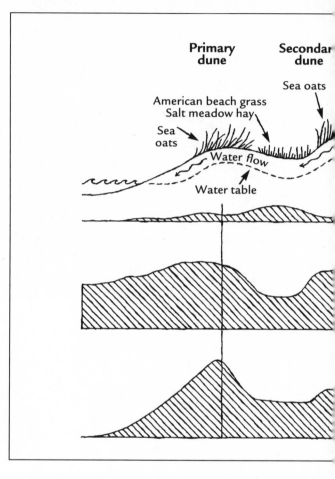

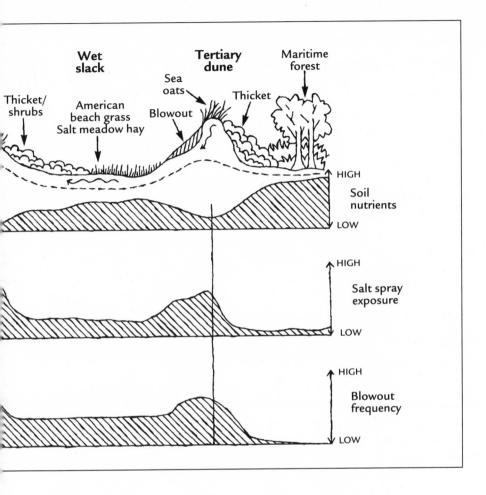

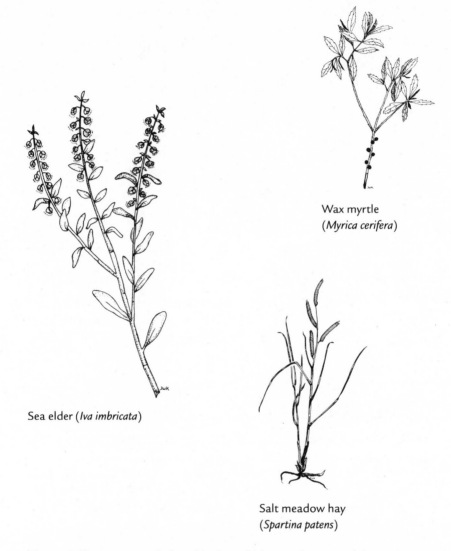

Wax myrtle
(*Myrica cerifera*)

Sea elder (*Iva imbricata*)

Salt meadow hay
(*Spartina patens*)

Figure 16. Plants commonly found in dune thickets and protected dune areas.
From E. Jean Wilson Kraus, *A Guide to Ocean Dune Plants Common to North Carolina*
(Chapel Hill: University of North Carolina Press, 1988).

Bluestem
(*Andropogon
scoparius*)

Groundsel, cottonbush
(*Baccharis halimifolia*)

Yaupon (*Ilex vomitoria*)

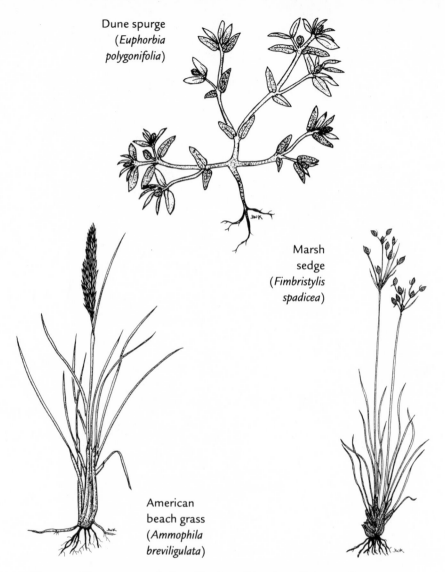

Dune spurge
(*Euphorbia
polygonifolia*)

Marsh
sedge
(*Fimbristylis
spadicea*)

American
beach grass
(*Ammophila
breviligulata*)

Figure 17. Plants commonly found in dune flats. From E. Jean Wilson Kraus, *A Guide to Ocean Dune Plants Common to North Carolina* (Chapel Hill: University of North Carolina Press, 1988).

Fire-wheel, Indian blanket
(*Gaillardia pulchella*)

Seaside goldenrod
(*Solidago sempervirens*)

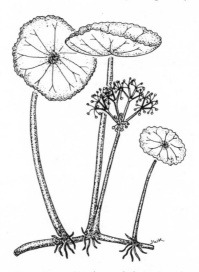

Pennywort (*Hydrocotyle bonariensis*)

A

Figure 18. Plant growth is modified by wind and salt exposure.
(A) "Flagged" live oak in the graveyard at Salvo Campground.
(B) "Wedged" thicket.
(C) Maritime forest growing below and behind Run Hill.
Photographs by author.

and of low diversity. Only 10 percent of its reptiles and amphibians are mainland types.

Maritime forests are the most stable areas of the Outer Banks. They have relatively well-developed soils, contain many plants and animals, and offer protection from salt spray and overwash. Early settlers recognized these advantages and built their houses in the forests. Many modern residents have done the same. Maritime forests make good places to live — for plants, for animals, and for people.

B

C

Deposition in the Sounds behind the Barriers

The Outer Banks would not be islands were it not for the sounds that separate them from the mainland. The beaches, dunes, and maritime forests of the Outer Banks cannot be fully understood without some knowledge of the environmental processes operating within the broad bodies of water that lie to the west and north. One of the most dramatic impacts of the sounds on the Banks is their ability to bring about winter snows. In both 1989 and 1994, cold fronts approaching from the west absorbed enough moisture from Pamlico Sound to cause several inches of snow to fall on the Banks. The process is essentially the same as the extraction of moisture from Lake Erie that produces snow in Buffalo. In the Great Lakes region, this is called the lake effect. On the Outer Banks, it should be called the sound effect for the loud rejoicing of children and the adult wails of dismay when the snows fall. The sounds affect both the water content and the temperature of the air moving across them. Snow is one manifestation of this influence. The exchange of heat and moisture with the sound waters plays a major role in reducing the temperature range on the Banks. Thus, the winters are warmer and the summers are cooler than on the mainland.

Water from the sounds also affects the Outer Banks directly. The most dramatic impact of sound waters on the Banks is the flooding that opens inlets after major storms move past the Banks, which has been previously discussed. Lesser flooding, as well as waves, can also have an impact. Sound-side erosion has increasingly become a concern as dune construction and stabilization have reduced sand movement across the Banks. Before human interference, sand was carried by wind and overwash to the sound-side beaches. Much of that sand has now been trapped by artificial dunes and residential development. As a result, sound-side beaches are being eroded by waves created by southwest winds blowing across the sounds. This problem is relatively minor when compared to oceanside beach erosion but is still significant in places that face the open waters of Pamlico and Albemarle sounds. Geologists refer to islands that are eroding from both sides as "narrowing in place." The fact that this process is occurring along the Outer Banks is not encouraging for their long-term future.

Another contribution the sounds make to the Banks is biological. The sounds have provided seafood for humans on the Banks since prehistoric times. Captain Arthur Barlowe's first view of Native Americans was of a fisherman filling his canoe "as deepe as it could swimme" with fish. Later Barlowe was entertained by a Roanoke chief who provided a meal that featured boiled and roasted fish along with venison, wheat cereal, melons, roots, and fruit. Native Americans were quite adept at capturing seafood from the sounds. The drawings made by John White in the summer of 1585 show Native Americans catching fish with weirs, traps, pounds, spears, and gigs. The fish in the illustrations appear to be eels, rays, sturgeons, croakers, gars, drums, bluefish, trout, and diamondback terrapins. White's drawings also show fish being roasted over an open fire and cooked in a stew with clams. Many of the fish first caught by Native Americans in the sixteenth century are still caught today. Colonists learned to catch fish from Native Americans, and over 400 years, Outer Bankers have continued to modify their methods to achieve quite amazing efficiency. The downside of these improvements was first demonstrated early in the twentieth century, when access to new markets, the Bankers' extensive knowledge of fish resources, and efficient harvesting techniques led to catch rates that drove sturgeons, diamondback terrapins, porpoises, coastal whales, and sea turtles to the brink of extinction. Overharvesting remains a problem today, even though environmental management efforts seek to optimize harvests while sustaining resources.

The productivity of the sounds is the result of the interaction of physical and chemical processes that trap organic and nutrient materials in the sounds rather than transporting them out to sea. These storage processes rely on the back-and-forth movement of sound waters by tides and winds. This oscillating flow keeps both water and dissolved materials in the sounds for long periods of time. Scientists refer to this as a long "residence time" in the sounds. The sounds also hold many chemicals "in residence." Freshwater runoff transports materials from upland areas to the sounds, and tidal flows bring materials from the sea. Once in the sounds, chemicals attach to particles that aggregate to form organic-rich mud that settles to the sound floor. Large quantities of organic matter and plant nutrients are trapped by this process, leading to high productivity in "estuarine nursery areas," where many aquatic animals congregate early in their life cycles. These productive nursery area waters are shallow, floored with organic-rich muds, and relatively protected from predators. Their ecological importance is revealed by the fact that regulations prohibit all fishing activities within them.

Unfortunately, the same environmental physics and chemistry that trap and store food for fish in the sounds also trap less desirable materials. The natural process that creates biological nurseries for fish also traps unwanted man-made materials such as pesticides, metals, industrial chemicals, and even excess nutrients from sewage treatment plants. Geologists and chemists at East Carolina University have located many areas within the sounds where concentrations of heavy metals like lead, tin, and cadmium are hundreds of times higher than normal levels. Fortunately, most of these areas are small, but their existence serves as a warning that modern society must do a better job of waste disposal if it hopes to preserve the productivity of nearshore waters.

CHAPTER TWO

GUIDE TO FIELD SITES

COROLLA TO OCRACOKE

This chapter identifies specific places you can visit to see evidence of the environmental processes described in Chapter 1. All of the sites in this field guide are open to the public, although some, such as Nags Head Woods Ecological Preserve, are open only at specific times. Some sites are areas of geologic interest (old inlets, modern inlets, overwash deposits, dune migration sites), whereas others are areas of biological interest (dunes, grass habitats, thickets, maritime forests, nature trails, wildlife refuges). Along the way, locations where interesting aspects of coastal currents and waves are likely to be seen will be pointed out (such as Cape Point, where different types of waves can be observed). This field guide is meant to be used after reading Chapter 1, but if you read the guide first, you might discover something that interests you, make your own observations, and then read the description in Chapter 1 to see if it agrees with your observations. Natural science proceeds from specific observation to general explanation (theory) via the process of discovery. Try the procedure for yourself; you might enjoy it.

To help you locate the sites, mileages to the north and south of Whalebone Junction are provided. Whalebone Junction is the intersection where US 64, 264, and 158 meet NC 12 south of Nags Head. This intersection can be confusing because US 158 as well as US 64 and 264 originate here, and thus NC 12 is the only road that continues north and south of the junction. The milepost signs between Kitty Hawk and Nags Head are also referenced. South of Salvo, distances are provided from Salvo and the

Buxton post office, then from the ferry docks in Ocracoke and Hatteras and the post office in Ocracoke.

The field guide is divided into six regions: Whalebone Junction to Corolla; Whalebone Junction to Rodanthe; Rodanthe to Canadian Hole near Buxton; Hatteras Island; Hatteras/Ocracoke ferry; and Ocracoke Island. The environmental processes described in Chapter 1 can be explored within each of these regions. Finally, some worthwhile side trips are noted after the discussion of primary sites within each region.

Whalebone Junction to Corolla

The Outer Banks north of Whalebone Junction have been heavily developed to support vacation and tourism activities. This development began in the 1830s when a planter named Francis Nixon brought his family to Nags Head for the summer "to breathe the salt air and bathe in the ocean"—activities then believed to prevent malaria. By 1838, a 200-guest hotel had been built on the sound side of Nags Head that accommodated visitors from North Carolina, Virginia, and the northeastern United States. Most visitors came from North Carolina and Virginia, just as they do today.

Although residential development of the northern Outer Banks has reduced the number of places where natural processes can be observed, several sites remain, including Soundside Road in Nags Head; Ocean Bay Boulevard, Nags Head Woods Ecological Preserve, and Run Hill in Kill Devil Hills; the U.S. Army Corps of Engineers Coastal Engineering Research Center in Duck; and the Corolla Lighthouse and grounds (see figure 19).

Figure 19. Whalebone Junction to Corolla. Sites north of Duck are on the right-hand map; those to the south are on the left. Base map from National Oceanic and Atmospheric Administration, National Ocean Service Chart 12204.

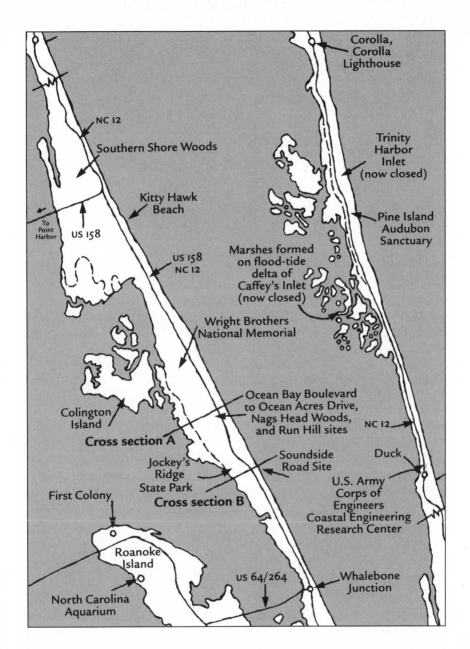

Corolla,
Corolla
Lighthouse

NC 12

Southern Shore Woods

Trinity
Harbor
Inlet
(now closed)

Kitty Hawk
Beach

Pine Island
Audubon
Sanctuary

To
Point
Harbor

US 158

US 158
NC 12

Marshes formed
on flood-tide
delta of
Caffey's Inlet
(now closed)

Wright Brothers
National Memorial

Colington
Island

Ocean Bay Boulevard
to Ocean Acres Drive,
Nags Head Woods,
and Run Hill sites

NC 12

Cross section A

Jockey's
Ridge
State Park

Soundside
Road Site

Duck

First Colony

Cross section B

U.S. Army
Corps of
Engineers
Coastal Engineering
Research Center

Roanoke
Island

North Carolina
Aquarium

US 64/264

Whalebone
Junction

Figure 19.
Cross sections.

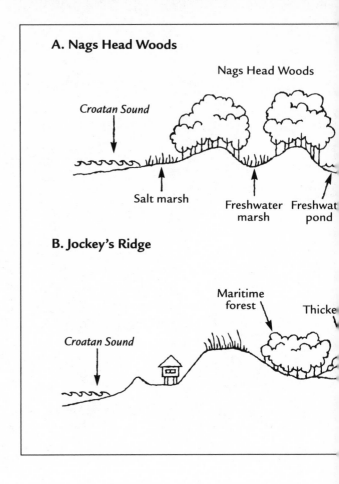

A. Nags Head Woods

Nags Head Woods

Croatan Sound

Salt marsh

Freshwater marsh

Freshwater pond

B. Jockey's Ridge

Maritime forest

Thicket

Croatan Sound

Soundside Road

Soundside Road, 3.6 miles from Whalebone Junction at milepost 13, is of interest for four reasons: the "unpainted aristocracy," the nickname for the shingled nineteenth-century beach cottages that represent the first shoreside development on the Outer Banks; the "flats," a well-drained thicket (once forest) where Bankers farmed before the land became too valuable; Jockey's Ridge, an active sand dune that is being driven south-

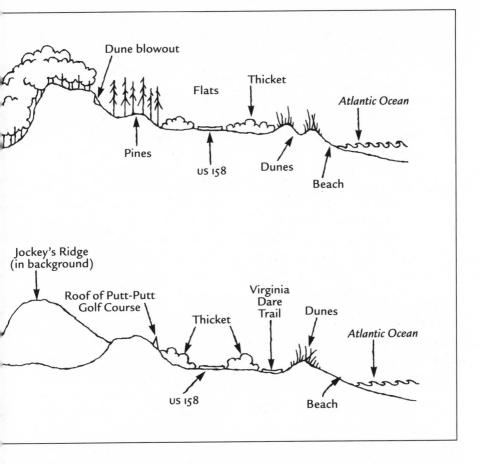

westward into a residential neighborhood; and the sound-side beach along the less-visited side of Jockey's Ridge State Park.

The "unpainted aristocracy" are the oldest summer cottages on the Outer Banks, some dating back to the 1830s. All of the oldest cottages have been moved to the ocean side because before the 1880s houses were not constructed on the oceanfront. W. G. Pool, a physician from Elizabeth City, built the first cottage on this oceanfront in 1884. Nags Head had become a leading seashore resort in the mid-1850s. Early visitors had followed the lead of prior inhabitants and built their cottages and hotels as far back from the ocean as possible. Pool began a new trend by building his house on the shore and encouraging others to do so by giving 130-foot-wide building lots to his friends' wives. About forty of the cottages built during this period remain today. Most are now set on pilings to allow waves and sand to pass beneath them. Many still have latticework around the piles — a decorative feature now but originally an important functional one, as it kept cattle, sheep, and pigs from seeking shade under the houses.

The "flats" between the coastal road (Virginia Dare Trail) and highway 158/12, as their name suggests, are relatively flat areas once covered with trees that were cleared for farming in the eighteenth century. These areas are now sites for residential and commercial development. A few patches of thicket dominated by wax myrtle (also called southern bayberry because it bears waxy gray berries along its stem), groundsel (sometimes called cottonbush for its white, fluffy autumn seed heads), dune elder, and yaupon holly have returned on vacant lots but not to an extent that makes the thickets useful for nature study.

Jockey's Ridge, the largest natural sand dune on the Outer Banks, lies just north of West Soundside Road and west of highway 158/12. The main body of the dune is to the north, but the extent of the dunefield and its actively depositing southwest faces are best seen from West Soundside Road. Several active faces occur near highway 158/12, but the best place to see them is about ¼ mile further west. Here the roadside is wide enough for parking and the dune is close enough to climb. If you climb the dune, you will be able to see the peak of Jockey's Ridge to the north, with its hang-gliding schools and sand boarders, but you will be far enough away to enjoy the natural dunescape without disturbing these recreational activities.

On the southwest side of Jockey's Ridge, the active face of the dune is encroaching on a maritime forest and the backyards of two houses. This land is to be purchased for the state park. If you walk to the edge of the steeply angled downwind dune face, you can watch your footsteps start small cascades of sand down the face, thereby demonstrating the phenomenon known to geologists as the "angle of repose," that is, the maximum angle at which sediment particles of specific size and composition can be piled. Your disturbance of this dune face will not change its angle. Sand will cascade down, but the angle will be reestablished before the motion stops. On windy days, sand moves over the dune surface and is deposited on the downwind side at the angle of repose. In this instance, sand carried by winds reaches the active dune face and cascades down into the forest and yards below. If the wind blows from some other direction, sand will move to the dune crest, or to something else that interferes with its movement, and will accumulate on the downwind side of it. Geologists attribute the large size of some dunes along the northern Outer Banks to the alternating windfield (see figures 4 and 5). It is clear from West Soundside Road that the dominant winds on Jockey's Ridge are from the northeast, but the dunes wouldn't be as high as they are if southwest winds didn't also help build them.

Homeowners near these dunes must deal with the consequences of dune activity. Nothing short of extensive plantings or trucking sand away can halt the dunes' movement. Both methods have been used to "stabilize" the dunes on the Banks. The dune at the Wright Brothers National Memorial at Kill Devil Hills has been stabilized by covering it with trucked-in topsoil planted with Bermuda wire grass, bitter tanic, and native thicket shrubs. Sand from a large dune near Corolla known as Poyner Hill has been moved to construction sites and now exists only as a "landmark" on government navigation charts.

At the western end of Soundside Road, a parking lot provides access to the sound-side beach, the shallow waters beyond, and a back entrance to Jockey's Ridge State Park. The main entrance to the park and to its two major nature trails is located on the north side of Jockey's Ridge off of highway 158/12.

Virginia Dare Trail north of Soundside Road passes by more of the "unpainted aristocracy" and allows travelers to see several shoreline areas that have been overwashed by storm waves. The sand removed in these events built the mid-island "flats." Beach erosion is also fairly intense along this section, demonstrating historical evidence that the beaches are eroding at the average rate of 4–5 feet per year. Travelers on the shore road can also see another Outer Banks specialty, a shipwreck site. The wreck of the U.S. man-of-war *Huron*, an iron steam vessel that went aground in 1877 with the loss of ninety-eight lives, lies just offshore of East Bladen Street near milepost 13. An information kiosk at a beach access ramp describes the wreck of the *Huron*. Those who want to know more about the incident can find a detailed account in David Stick's book, *Graveyard of the Atlantic* (1952). The remains of the wreck are sometimes visible at low tide when the offshore sandbars are spaced just right. Shoreward-moving bars have been continuously covering and uncovering the ship since it wrecked in 1877.

Ocean Bay Boulevard, Nags Head Woods Ecological Preserve, and Run Hill

The Kill Devil Hills beach access area at Ocean Bay Boulevard (8.2 miles from Whalebone Junction, about milepost 8.4) is a good spot from which to begin a crossing of the Banks ending up in Nags Head Woods Ecological Preserve — the five-star nature event in this area. The beach access area at Ocean Bay Boulevard has ample parking, a boardwalk leading to the beach, a bathhouse, and noteworthy dune and beach areas. The beach is steep and composed of relatively coarse sand above the mid-tide level. Below the mid-tide line, the beach is usually flat and composed of medium to fine sand. The beach sand is of striking contrast in particle size to the fine, wind-driven grains found in the dunes. Because of the difference in beach steepness above and below the mid-tide level, a number of different types of breakers can usually be observed here (see figure 6).

The coastal dune at this site supports a surprisingly diverse array of plant life. Besides the ubiquitous sea oats (*Uniola paniculata*), American beach grass (*Ammophila breviligulata*), and salt meadow cordgrass (*Spartina patens*), other plants that thrive there include pennywort (*Hydrocotyle bonariensis*), seaside evening primrose (*Oenothera humifusa*), golden aster (*Heterotheca subaxillaris*), fire-wheel (*Gaillardia pulchella*), seaside goldenrod (*Solidago sempervirens*), and dune spurge (*Euphorbia polygonifolia*). (For descriptions of these plants, see E. Jean Wilson Kraus, *A Guide to Ocean Dune Plants Common to North Carolina* [1988], published for the University of North Carolina Sea Grant College Program and generally available at

Outer Banks bookstores, including the one at the nearby Wright Brothers National Memorial.)

The recommended route across the Banks is Ocean Acres Drive (1 mile south of the Kill Devil Hills beach access area), which intersects North Virginia Dare Trail at a sign reading "To 158." Travel south for half a block on highway 158/12, then turn right onto West Ocean Acres Drive (milepost 9.5). This road passes through a residentially developed pine forest, continues steeply uphill over a dune ridge, then plunges down into Nags Head Woods. This 1,400-acre maritime forest of oaks, gums, maples, and hollies has relatively few live oaks and loblolly pines—trees commonly found in most other Outer Banks forests. The forest is so rare that the U.S. Congress designated it a national natural landmark in 1974, and the North Carolina chapter of the Nature Conservancy made it one of its first protection projects in 1977. The Nature Conservancy has now acquired 420 acres of the forest itself, owns another 390 acres jointly with the town of Nags Head, and leases yet another 300 acres from the town. The preserve contains miles of well-marked nature trails that begin at the interpretive center at 701 West Ocean Acres Drive. The Nature Conservancy also offers guided field trips and children's nature camps during the summer. Visiting hours vary with the season; for information on programs and trail access, call 919-441-2525. Even if you are unable to arrange a visit at a time when the interpretive center and the nature trails that start there are open, it is worth seeing the woods from the road or from another trail that begins at Nags Head Town Park on West Barnes Street at milepost 11. The public road past the interpretive center on West Ocean Acres Drive ends at Boundary Road at the Nags Head Sanitation Service sign. If you turn right, you can drive about a mile through the Nags Head Woods to West Martin Street.

The biota of Nags Head Woods is exceptionally diverse for a barrier island maritime forest. Eleven species of oaks, 10 ferns, 3 pines, 2 magnolias, 2 cedars, 2 willows, 5 milkweeds, 4 goldenrods, and 3 cattails are found among the more than 300 species of plants identified so far. Over 100 species of birds, 65 species of land vertebrates (amphibians, reptiles, and mammals), and 6 species of freshwater fish also live there. This extraordinary diversity is made possible by the unusual protection from salt spray afforded by tall dune ridges that surround the forest on three sides. Low water-filled areas between these dunes add aquatic and edge habitat to the forest habitat. A forest that would be fascinating in any setting, Nags Head Woods is an extraordinarily interesting barrier island forest — a "must visit" site for anyone exploring barrier island ecology.

After leaving the Nature Conservancy property on West Martin Street, turn left onto Ninth Avenue, turn left again onto West Air Strip Road, and continue until you reach the foot of the Run Hill dunefield. After parking along the road, you can climb Run Hill near its southern border with Nags Head Woods. As you climb the northeast face of the dune, note its steepness and loose sand, and after you reach the dune crest, note that the southwest face of the dune is equally steep and uncompacted. You will have just examined physical evidence that records the two prevailing wind directions on the Outer Banks — southwest and northeast. The northeast depositing dune face that you climbed was formed by southwest winds, and the southwest dune face moving into Nags Head Woods was formed by northeast winds. Note also the sand-trapping ability of dune vegetation; sea oats and American beach grass crown the top of the dune hummocks, trailing sand ridges behind them. These ridges record the fact that the strongest prevailing winds are from the northeast.

The most dramatic views from the crest of Run Hill are to the south toward Nags Head Woods and to the southwest across forest, thicket, freshwater marsh, salt marsh, and Roanoke Sound to Roanoke Island 3.5 miles in the distance (see figure 20). This vantage point helps explain why the forest at Nags Head Woods is so well protected from salt spray. Run Hill itself forces salt-laden winds to rise above the forest canopy along the southwestern edge of the dunefield, and Roanoke Island protects the woods from spray produced by large waves in Albemarle and Pamlico sounds. The other two sides of the protective box around Nags Head Woods are made up of the tall dune ridge you crossed on the way to and from the Nature Conservancy tract and Jockey's Ridge. Together, these features protect the woods from salt spray and have allowed the development of a diverse forest far more typical of coastal plain or piedmont forests than of other barrier island forests.

Figure 20. Dunes protect plants from salt spray: view from Run Hill to the southwest. Note the forest below the dune crest, thickets and marshes in the middistance, and Roanoke Island on the horizon. Photograph by Watts Hill, Jr.

Wright Brothers National Memorial

The Wright Brothers National Memorial is worth a visit even though its natural setting has been altered. Topsoil was added to the dune's surface in the 1920s, and the entire dune was seeded with plants the National Park Service identifies as Bermuda wire grass and bitter tanic. The extent of these changes is readily apparent if you compare today's grassy setting to photographs of the bare sand the Wright brothers encountered.

Visitors to the memorial can learn important lessons about science and technology. Environmental conditions on the Outer Banks played a role in the Wright brothers' success; a relatively predictable sea breeze blowing up a treeless slope made the site an ideal place to learn to fly—an advantage grasped today by hang-gliding schools on Jockey's Ridge. The Wright brothers succeeded at manned flight because of three technical breakthroughs. First, they discovered through experiments in their wind tunnel and with their gliders at Kitty Hawk that existing calculations of the lift produced by various wing shapes were too high by a factor of 1.67. They therefore concluded that the wing size for an effective flying machine had to be much larger than had previously been calculated. Second, they learned from watching gliding birds like gulls, ospreys, and pelicans that stable turns were accomplished by "banking," the same method a bicycle rider uses to maintain stability in a turn. As a result, the Wrights controlled their machines by twisting the wood and canvas wings to achieve a banked turn. Third, they used their newly calculated lift ratios to design a propeller that was more powerful than any others in existence. Powered, manned flight would not have been possible without all three of these breakthroughs. The fact that all three were made as a result of the unlikely combination of Ohio bicycle shop owners and field experiments on the Outer Banks fully justifies a visit to the site of their success. The memorial's museum provides excellent displays illustrating the brothers' progress and achievements, and live demonstrations with a full-scale model of the first flying machine make their wing-twisting method for achieving banked turns absolutely unforgettable.

Side Trips: Colington Island, Kitty Hawk Beach, Southern Shore Woods

Several worthwhile side trips can be taken within residential developments on the northern Outer Banks. Although part of the fun of a visit is exploring on your own, three short trips are recommended.

First, just south of the Wright Brothers National Memorial, Colington Road leads west to Colington Island. This island has a number of seafood shops, including several crab-shedding operations. Crab shedding is the process whereby blue crabs are collected after molting. The crabs are watched carefully to determine when they molt and then removed from seawater within 20 minutes of shedding their old shells. They are then sold as soft-shelled crabs, a great delicacy. Visitors can also observe new bridge approaches built with sand from ancient dune ridges (see figure 21) and the results of residential development that has proceeded without centralized planning.

Second, a side trip along Virginia Dare Trail just east of the Kitty Hawk post office at milepost 4.2 is educational for its lessons about the consequences of building houses close to an eroding shoreline. At any given time, several houses are usually in the process of falling into the sea along this stretch of beach (see figure 22). The unobstructed view of the ocean in some places is mute evidence of shorefront houses that have already been destroyed. Almost all houses built seaward of Virginia Dare Trail here are at risk of a similar fate. A $12 million addition of sand to this beach has been proposed as a short-term solution to this problem.

Third, Southern Shore Woods, a residentially developed forest once similar to Nags Head Woods, can be reached by taking NC 12 about 2 miles north of its northern intersection with US 158 and then turning onto West Dogwood Trail. West Dogwood Trail passes over a dune ridge and into a well-developed maritime forest of oaks (red, white, and live), beeches, maples, and hollies. The road crosses a creek with bulkheaded banks before merging with South Dogwood Trail, which passes a marina and golf course before merging with US 158 just west of its intersection with NC 12. The circuit illustrates planned residential development in an Outer Banks maritime forest.

U.S. Army Corps of Engineers
Coastal Engineering Research Center

The U.S. Army Corps of Engineers Coastal Engineering Research Center is located 4.9 miles north of US 158 on NC 12. The center occupies a relatively undeveloped plot of land stretching completely across the bank. At this site, scientists conduct important research on the sand movement in the coastal ocean. It has a state-of-the-art wave-monitoring system and one of the longest existing records of wave size, frequency, and direction—or wave climate—in the world. It also has a wonderful Rube Goldberg–type machine called the CRAB (for Coastal Research Access Buggy), which crawls along the seafloor, as its name suggests, while scientists measure beach slope, sand movement, and offshore seafloor topography. Usually the CRAB is parked south of the center, its yellow tripod structure looming high above the center's roofline. During the summer, the center offers guided tours beginning at 10 A.M. to explain its research program and answer visitors' questions. An information kiosk to the left of the entrance

road provides information on waves, geological beach processes, wave-seafloor interaction, and shoreline engineering. The natural dunes, thickets, and wetlands on the grounds are easier to visit here than almost anywhere else in this residentially developed area. Within the dunes and wetlands, visitors can examine the stabilizing effect of artificially dense plantings of dune and wetland grasses. Ample paved parking is available near the information kiosk, and the entrance to a beach trail can be found at the east side of the parking area.

North of Duck: Observations in Transit to Corolla

Just north of Duck, the island shrinks to less than $1/10$ of a mile wide. This is a good spot from which to observe the narrow sound-side marshes at Sanderling and the much broader and extensive marshes to the north. The narrow marshes are dominated by the common reed *Phragmites australis*. The broad marshes beyond have zones of plant growth with smooth cordgrass (*Spartina alterniflora*) at the water's edge, black needlerush (*Juncus roemerianus*) in the middle, and a combination of *Phragmites* and cattail (*Typha* spp.) at the landward margin. Currituck Sound has become a freshwater sound since the closing of New Currituck Inlet in 1828. Freshwater marsh plants like *Phragmites* and others are important providers of energy in a food chain that includes bass and waterfowl. The broad marshes north of Sanderling, however, owe their existence to the ocean. They are growing on sediment deposited on the old flood-tide delta of Caffey's Inlet. (For more details on inlet processes, see Chapter 1 and the discussion of Oregon Inlet below.)

North of the Currituck County line, the National Audubon Society has established a bird sanctuary on a 2-mile stretch of undeveloped land called the Pine Island Audubon Sanctuary. The story behind the acquisition of the land in the mid-1970s is described in chapter 5 of Thomas J. Schoenbaum's book, *Islands, Capes, and Sounds: The North Carolina Coast* (1982). It is a tale full of venality and political intrigue, in which develop-

Figure 21. Where have all the old dunes gone? Sand removed from an old dune at Colington was used in the construction of bridge ramps in 1994. Photographs by author.

Figure 22. Building houses on dunes is risky. Oceanfront houses damaged by overwash at Kitty Hawk, 1994. Photograph by author.

ers and environmentalists laboriously worked out an agreement only to have it vetoed by James Watt, the secretary of interior in the first Reagan administration. The agreement included plans for the creation of a large wildlife refuge and for clustered residential development on the Banks north of Duck. Visitors can judge the relative merits of the development that occurred without the plan and the clustered development and wildlife refuge that would have occurred under the agreement.

Corolla Lighthouse

About the only unposted natural land accessible to the public north of Duck is the one-block-wide stretch from ocean to sound at the Corolla Lighthouse. The habitat is fairly typical: small seaside dunes front a thicket on the ocean side of the road, and a live oak/pine maritime forest grades to freshwater marsh on the sound side. The site is too small to provide much diversity, but the well-preserved lighthouse is a treat to see. A pleasant boardwalk traversing the marsh makes it possible to observe the red maples (*Acer rubrum*), water oaks (*Quercus nigra*), swamp rose (*Rosa palustris*), cattails (*Typha latifolia* and *angustifolia*), and marsh elder (*Iva frutescens*) that dominate this productive community. Note especially the tall cattails and reeds that grow here. All the plant material in this marsh grows in one season, making it a real productivity powerhouse. It is little wonder that Currituck Sound is known nationally for its largemouth bass fishing. The productivity that supports the bass population can be seen from the boardwalk.

The small town of Corolla is one of several villages that grew up around nineteenth-century U.S. Life-Saving Service stations. One of the life-saving stations, moved to Corolla from further south, now serves as the office for a real estate company.

One of the more interesting natural phenomena you can still observe in Corolla is the wild horse herd. Genetic studies of these horses support the lore that they are descended from horses brought to the New World by Spanish explorers. Studies by the equine genetics program at the University of Kentucky show that the blood groups of the Corolla horses are more closely linked to Spanish horses than are the blood groups of any other wild horse herd in North America. Although these horses eat better now that humans have planted lawns and shrubs where there used to be only dunes, they face the threat of death by automobile. More than a dozen horses have been killed by automobiles in the last decade.

Before you leave Corolla, if you have a four-wheel-drive vehicle or can gain access to one, drive north along the beach to the Virginia border. Development along this stretch, which can only be reached by driving on the beach, strains one's credulity (see figure 23). You will see million-dollar houses with indoor swimming pools; free-range American bison grazing placidly on the sand dunes; and several beach houses built so close to the ocean that more than half of each structure extends over the beach, with the remaining foundation protected by gigantic sandbags—a state-approved "temporary" solution to an "emergency" erosion problem. You will also see stumps of still-rooted live oak trees standing in the surf at

Figure 23.
Development north of
Corolla. Photographs
by author.

mid-tide level—sure evidence that the island is moving landward out from under a forest—and a fence with a locked gate preventing vehicular access to the generally "public" wet sand beach between high and low tide at Virginia's False Cape State Park and the Back Bay National Wildlife Refuge.

Whalebone Junction to Rodanthe

Much less residential development has occurred south of Whalebone Junction than north of it. In fact, the route south to Rodanthe passes

through two areas of prime waterfowl habitat, over one active inlet, and past the sites of six closed inlets. This stretch of the Cape Hatteras National Seashore also offers two informative nature trails. The areas covered in this section are Coquina Beach, Bodie Island Lighthouse, and Bodie Island Dike Nature Trail; Oregon Inlet; and Pea Island National Wildlife Refuge (see figure 24).

An information center on NC 12 immediately south of its intersection with US 158 has brochures on the Cape Hatteras National Seashore and usually has on-site personnel to provide information on road conditions (NC 12 is sometimes closed), answer questions, and suggest places to visit. Just south of the information center, you will see large freshwater marshes and ponds on the west side of the road. These developed on top of the flood-tide delta deposits of four old inlets—Roanoke, Gunt, Hattorask, and Port Lane. Although thickets sometimes block the view of the entire width of the Banks here, the old inlet sediments have combined to make Bodie Island over a mile wide at this point.

Roanoke Inlet, which closed about 1800, is the most famous of the four inlets because most historians believe it provided access to Roanoke Island when settlers sent by Sir Walter Raleigh established the first English-speaking colony there in 1585. Gunt Inlet, 2 miles further south, was smaller and shorter-lived, opening in the 1730s and closing in the 1770s. Hattorask and Port Lane inlets existed from before 1585 until the 1650s and were located south of Gunt Inlet.

The flood-tide deltas of these four inlets have provided low, water-saturated land ideal for waterfowl habitat. Hunters have long used these lands and continue to do so as a pre-existing use of land that is now part of Cape Hatteras National Seashore. The area provides habitat for thousands of geese (Canadian and snow), tundra swans, ducks, herons, egrets, ibis, pelicans, coots, gallinules, shearwaters, gulls, terns, and other species too numerous to mention. Bird-watching platforms are located at several points along the road, as are recently renovated hunting blinds that can be reserved in hunting season by contacting the Enforcement Section of

Figure 24. Whalebone Junction to Rodanthe. Base map from National Oceanic and Atmospheric Administration, National Ocean Service Chart 12204.

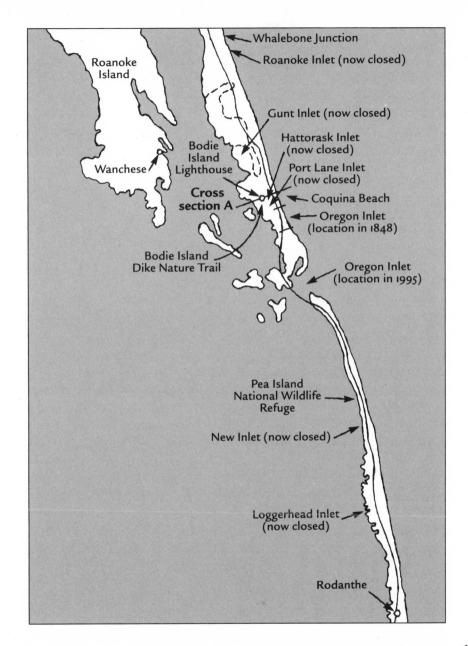

Roanoke Island

Whalebone Junction

Roanoke Inlet (now closed)

Gunt Inlet (now closed)

Bodie Island Lighthouse

Hattorask Inlet (now closed)

Wanchese

Port Lane Inlet (now closed)

Cross section A

Coquina Beach

Oregon Inlet (location in 1848)

Bodie Island Dike Nature Trail

Oregon Inlet (location in 1995)

Pea Island National Wildlife Refuge

New Inlet (now closed)

Loggerhead Inlet (now closed)

Rodanthe

Figure 24.
Cross section.

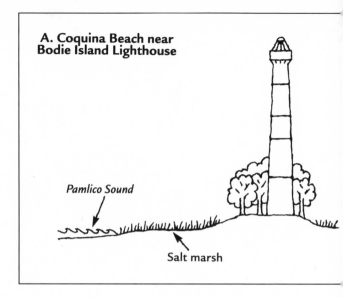

A. Coquina Beach near Bodie Island Lighthouse

Pamlico Sound

Salt marsh

the National Seashore (Route 1, Box 675, Manteo, NC 27954; 919-473-2111). A good bird identification book such as John Fussell's *A Birder's Guide to Coastal North Carolina* or Roger Tory Peterson's *A Field Guide to the Birds* as well as rubber boots, binoculars, and insect repellent are recommended accessories for those who utilize these platforms and blinds.

Coquina Beach, Bodie Island Lighthouse, and Bodie Island Dike Nature Trail

South of Whalebone Junction 5.3 miles, a crossroad leads to Coquina Beach on the ocean side and Bodie Island Lighthouse and Bodie Island Dike Nature Trail on the sound side. Both sides of the road are worth exploring.

The road to Coquina Beach leads to a parking lot behind hummocky dunes and the remains of the *Laura A. Barnes*, a four-masted wooden schooner that wrecked here in 1921. The remains are located on the landward side of what remains of a man-made primary dune — an indication

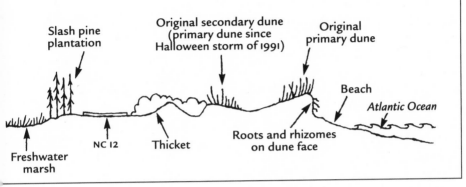

Slash pine plantation

Original secondary dune (primary dune since Halloween storm of 1991)

Original primary dune

Beach

Atlantic Ocean

NC 12

Thicket

Roots and rhizomes on dune face

Freshwater marsh

of where the beach was located in 1921, before the artificial dunes were built. North of the *Laura A. Barnes* is a prime example of dune overwash and the damage it can do to coastal construction. The bathhouse is closed for reasons that become apparent as you walk north. A major dune over-wash event occurred here during the Halloween storm of 1991, washing away the seawardmost section of what was once a loop road to the old Coast Guard station and burying the access ramps to the bathhouse in sand. The origin of the sand that caused the damage is readily apparent when you look toward the beach and see the concrete remains of the septic tanks that were once buried within the primary dune. The dune was destroyed by the overwash event, and the sand from it was washed over the road, into the bathhouse and the thicket habitat beyond. Further evidence of this sand movement can be seen as you walk toward the old Coast Guard station. What was once a continuous line of primary dunes is now represented by two or three hummocky dunes with severely eroded faces on all but the inland side. Here, a long ridge of sand has been formed by northeast winds. Still further north, you will find the loop road blocked by windblown sand to a depth of more than 20 feet (see figure 25).

The beach access facilities at Coquina Beach have not been repaired in keeping with National Park Service management policy stating that "natural shoreline processes (erosion, deposition, dune formation, inlet formation, and shoreline migration) that are not influenced by human actions will be allowed to continue without abatement except where control measures are required by law. . . . Managers will plan to phase out, relocate, or provide alternative facilities for park developments located in hazardous areas that cannot reasonably be protected." Further south, however, dune overwash has been repaired at sites where North Carolina has a legal right to protect the transportation infrastructure (NC 12 and the Herbert C. Bonner Bridge over Oregon Inlet) and where the National Park Service is obligated to protect significant cultural resources (Cape Hatteras Lighthouse).

The road to Bodie Island Lighthouse and the Bodie Island Dike Nature Trail is directly across NC 12 from the road to Coquina Beach. The road is flanked by nonnative slash pine planted in the early twentieth century and natural thickets growing within the protection of these trees. Mid-nineteenth-century maps of this area reveal that it was dominated by sand flats, grasslands, and marshes. The existing lighthouse was built in 1872, earlier versions having been built on the same site in 1848 and 1859. The purpose of the lighthouse was to mark the location of Oregon Inlet, now the only navigable access between sound and ocean between Chesapeake Bay and Cape Hatteras. This inlet opened during a hurricane in 1846 and was named after the first ship to pass through it.

The lighthouse is not open to visitors, but the parking area provides access to the Bodie Island Dike Nature Trail, reached by following the road at the southwest corner of the lighthouse loop road. The road to the trail is interesting. Not only does it pass through a classic thicket-to-salt-marsh transition, but it is made of Castle Hayne marl, a carbonate material containing fossilized clams over 20 million years old. About ¼ mile down this road is the entrance to the nature trail, where informative brochures are available. The trail is over 6 miles long and can be hot and buggy in summer. It is a loop trail, but you may wish to consider turning

Figure 25. Migrating dunes do not obey stop signs. Coquina Beach loop road covered by migrating dune. Photograph by author.

back before completing its full length. The trail features freshwater marshes (station 2), a stand of loblolly pines planted by the National Park Service in 1961 as part of an erosion control effort (station 3), a thicket (station 4), a diked area where freshwater habitats are located east of a plank-faced earthen dam (stations 5–6), and saltwater habitats to the west (stations 5–8). The trail provides excellent bird-watching opportunities and seems little used during the nonsummer months.

Interesting views from the trail are made more scenic by the sight of the lighthouse to the north and the bridge over Oregon Inlet to the south. Such views provide food for thought. All the land between the lighthouse and Oregon Inlet was built up by sand deposited in the inlet by along-shore transport since 1872. The Outer Banks are dynamic land forms, and no place is more dynamic than Oregon Inlet.

Oregon Inlet

Oregon Inlet opened on 7 September 1846 when water from the sound flooded through Bodie Island after a hurricane passed along the coast (see figure 2). It must have been quite a storm since it formed Hatteras Inlet the next day. Other inlets existed near Oregon Inlet when it opened in 1846, and, as already pointed out, still others had previously existed in the vicinity (Roanoke, Gunt, Hattorask, and Port Lane to the north, and New, Loggerhead, and Chickinacommock to the south; see figure 1). However, prior to September 1846, only one dependable inlet existed north of Cape Hatteras — New Inlet near Rodanthe. Oregon Inlet soon became the dominant navigation route through the northern Banks as New Inlet steadily shoaled before closing completely in the 1930s.

The five major features that should be examined at Oregon Inlet are the southward extension of Bodie Island into the inlet, evidenced by the series of old island ends preserved as dune ridges among the salt marshes under the causeway section of the Herbert C. Bonner Bridge; the extensive and complex flood-tide delta west of the bridge; the ebb-tide delta, represented by an arc of breakers extending from one side of the inlet to the other just offshore of the beach; evidence of erosion along the Pea Island shore of the inlet; and the swift tidal currents that sweep through the inlet, creating all of the inlet's other features. Unfortunately, these features are rarely observable simultaneously. Tidal currents are best observed at mid-tide levels, and tidal deltas are best seen at low tide. Furthermore, the ebb-tide delta is easiest to locate when onshore winds create breakers offshore, but under such conditions, the flood-tide delta shows up poorly. Nonetheless, this is the best Banks inlet to visit to observe inlet processes because of its dynamic character and navigational importance and because the Herbert C. Bonner Bridge makes an excellent observation platform. I drive class groups over the bridge and back at least twice, asking students to focus on one feature at a time until they are confident they have seen them all. Most readers will not be tested on this later, so you need not be that compulsive.

The features of Oregon Inlet are, of course, only specific examples of general features found in all barrier island inlets. Oregon Inlet is more dynamic than most, however, because more sand (500,000 to 1,000,000 cubic yards per year) moves past it. As a result, the inlet has moved southeast along the shore over 2 miles since 1846, and the entrance has moved landward over 1,800 feet during the same period.

The general features of tidal currents that pass through inlets and the ebb- and flood-tide deltas formed by the sediments they move were discussed in Chapter 1 (see figures 9 and 10). Inlet hydraulics is conceptually simple — large masses of water move onshore and offshore in response to rising and falling tides. These water masses move relatively slowly in open waters but speed up as they flow through narrow inlet openings between islands. Rapid currents erode sand from the sides and bottom of the inlet, but the sand sinks back to the seafloor when the currents slow. Deposition under slowing currents forms tidal deltas inside the inlet on rising tide (flood-tide delta) and outside the inlet on falling tide (ebb-tide delta). Alongshore transport of sand alters this general picture in Oregon Inlet by depositing more sand on one side of the inlet than on the other, causing the inlet to move toward the side receiving less sediment.

Oregon Inlet is moving south. Note that the bridge is attached to Bodie Island about 1 mile from the southern end, but it is attached to Pea Island almost at the northernmost point on the inshore side of the island. This was not always the case. Figure 26 compares the location of the bridge and the shoreline in 1965, 1 year after the bridge was completed, and in 1993, 28 years after construction. During this period, the north side of Oregon Inlet was filled in by 6/10 mile of deposited sand, while the south side moved south only about half as far. In 1993 the inlet was narrower and deeper than it was in 1965. Regularly dredging the inlet and building a "sand-retaining structure" at the north end of Pea Island have kept Pea Island from eroding as much as Bodie Island has extended. The sand-retaining structure was built to hold sand dredged from the inlet in a place where natural processes carry it along the beach of Pea Island. This system seems to work quite well and may serve as a substitute for the mile-long jetties planned by the U.S. Army Corps of Engineers as a way of "stabilizing" Oregon Inlet. These jetties would have extended past the tidal deltas outside the inlet, thereby improving navigation but blocking the natural transport of sand across the inlet. You can park at the foot of the bridge on Pea Island and see for yourself how the sand-retaining structure is working, but walking on the structure is prohibited.

Pea Island National Wildlife Refuge

Pea Island is home to a U.S. Fish and Wildlife Service wildlife refuge that extends from Oregon Inlet to the town of Rodanthe. Visitors are free to explore the refuge except for clearly marked nesting areas and areas containing stands of threatened or endangered plants; hunting is also prohibited. Much of the northern half of the refuge is managed to enhance its use by migratory waterfowl and other birds. About 14 miles south of Whalebone Junction (7 miles south of Oregon Inlet; 10 miles north of Rodanthe), a nature trail extends along a dike separating two freshwater ponds. The trail is worth visiting, both for bird-watching and for viewing the surrounding habitat. Field glass–equipped platforms are located every few hundred feet and informative signs are positioned along the trail, but a bird identification guide and your own binoculars will greatly enhance your appreciation of the waterfowl. John Fussell, a noted coastal birder, says this is the best available bird-watching site on the Outer Banks. Many more types of birds can be identified than the three — big brown birds, little brown birds, and seagulls — that a friend once told me were all-inclusive; but the different varieties of sandpipers, plovers, immature gulls and terns, and herons certainly are difficult to differentiate and require some time with a birder's guide to identify with confidence.

The nature trail extends for a 2-mile circuit along the sound side of one pond, but if you walk to and from the two-story platform at the end of the dike, you can observe most of the species generally present. The further you are from the trailhead, the more privacy you will have for longer, uninterrupted viewing, so let commitment to birding be your guide. It is useful to walk as far as the observation platform, because only from there can you see the extensive salt marsh on the sound side of Pea Island. The marsh here has a characteristic zonation pattern, with thicket plants along the base of the dike, followed by freshwater marsh plants (cattails, common reed) in the middle distance and salt marsh species (black needlerush, smooth cordgrass) near the creeks and sound. The change is

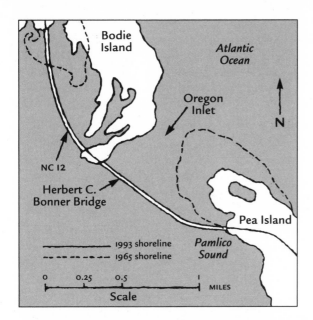

Figure 26. Oregon Inlet, 1965 and 1993. Location of Herbert C. Bonner Bridge and NC 12 relative to Oregon Inlet in 1965 and 1993. The inlet has moved southeast over a third of a mile in 28 years. It would have moved further had it not been deepened by dredging and held in place by a stone breakwater at the north end of Pea Island. Illustration by Phil Townsend, based on an aerial photograph from the National Oceanic and Atmospheric Administration (1963) and a Landsat image from the National Aeronautics and Space Administration (1993).

not uniform with distance. Marsh plants are extremely sensitive to immersion cycles, so small differences in the height of the marsh surface or the distance from a tidal creek alter zonation dramatically. This phenomenon is well illustrated in the marsh beyond the ponds. The zonation here is decidedly patchy, with thicket-covered high spots (hammocks) appearing among all types of marsh vegetation.

Fifteen miles south of Whalebone Junction, NC 12 crosses the site of the former New Inlet, an apt name because new inlets were formed here repeatedly between the 1730s and the 1930s. As you can see from the sandbagged dune line and overwashed sand near the highway, this site almost became an inlet again in the early 1990s. The North Carolina Department of Transportation is rebuilding the dunes here and removing sand from NC 12 in accordance with rights granted the department under the terms that established the Cape Hatteras National Seashore. The department plans to relocate and elevate this overwash- and inlet-prone stretch of NC 12.

The Pea Island refuge headquarters is located about 16 miles south of Whalebone Junction (8 miles north of Rodanthe). A brief stop will allow you to survey the site of New Inlet and the rebuilt dunes sprigged with dune grass just south of the beach access road. Stabilizing dunes by planting dune grass has been surprisingly effective. Much of the dune line here and in other overwash-prone areas throughout the Outer Banks has been stabilized in this manner since the 1930s, but the technique has recently been improved greatly as a result of research by scientists at North Carolina State University. A dune grass nursery on Bodie Island grows plants from seed for subsequent sprigging in dune restoration.

Just north of the Rodanthe town line, you will encounter another overwash-prone area, possibly the site of a former inlet named Chickinacommock. Some claim that Chickinacommock Inlet was merely another name for New Inlet; others think a separate inlet existed here. I support the latter view. The island is narrow, low, and flat at this point and looks remarkably like other sites of old inlets. Like those other sites, this area is very prone to overwash. The current dune line was rebuilt completely after the 1991 Halloween storm destroyed its predecessor. Local residents helped to further widen the dune line by placing their discarded Christmas trees along its back edge to trap sand. The technique worked well and solved two problems—the dead trees were disposed of without ending up in a landfill, and the dune line was strengthened without cost to the public. The practice was discontinued, however, because the U.S. Fish and Wildlife Service feared that the trees might interfere with sea turtle nesting.

Rodanthe to Canadian Hole near Buxton

The Outer Banks from Rodanthe to Buxton have a certain sameness about them. The beaches are excellent and relatively uncrowded, even in summer. As a result, the beachwear code is sometimes informal, even though the National Park Service is obliged to enforce the standards set forth in North Carolina's indecent exposure laws. The beaches between Rodanthe and Buxton, however, are shielded from the eyes of law enforcement officers and other travelers on NC 12 by as many as two dune lines built by the Civilian Conservation Corps in the 1930s. The dunes along this stretch have been overwashed in several areas, sometimes closing the highway. Palisade dunes were built over sand fences to defend the road. Behind the palisade dunes is a flat area with typical dune vegetation and encroaching thickets. The thickets in this area provide good examples of the impact of salt spray because many individual plants display the flagged growth form described in Chapter 1. In open areas, the thickets themselves show the effects of salt spray exposure, exhibiting a "wedged" cross-sectional shape with a low edge facing windward and gradually taller shrubs and small trees further back.

The sound side of the Banks in this area is more varied than the dunes and flats. The mid-island thickets grade into typical salt marshes in some areas and into groves of stunted pines and live oaks in others. These forests were homesteaded by European pioneers inhabiting this section of the Outer Banks. Modern construction, however, takes place very close to the ocean. The clear evidence of salt spray impact, overwash events, and flooding has often been discounted by those who have built oceanfront structures in Avon, Salvo, and Waves. Sometimes these houses have to be moved back to avoid destruction. The buildings that have survived longest along this section of the Banks are the old life-saving stations at Chicamacomico and Little Kinnakeet. These stations, which were built far back from the ocean and relatively low to the ground, have lasted more than a century. It is interesting to ponder whether late twentieth-century construction will survive a century of Outer Banks weather.

The Chicamacomico Life-Saving Station in Rodanthe is worth a visit. The station has been restored through local, state, and federal cooperation and houses a shipwreck museum. A wonderfully preserved rainwater cistern is a testimonial to the skill of nineteenth-century masons. The area was also the site of a Civil War battle known as the Chicamacomico Races. The battle took place on 5 October 1862, when two Union army regiments traveled from Hatteras Inlet to Chicamacomico to investigate Confederate troop movements. The Federals were chased back to Cape Hatteras Lighthouse by a Georgia regiment that had waded ashore at Live Oak Camp. Reports of the "hot sand and bright sun" suggest that it was probably good beach weather. Be that as it may, a forced 24-mile march through loose sand, while someone shoots at you from the rear and others try to land between you and safety, is enough to ruin anyone's enthusiasm for beaches, no matter how pleasant the weather.

Two sites between Rodanthe and Buxton characterize the area: wind-sculpted live oaks at Salvo Campground and shipwrecks, overwashes, and dunes south of Salvo (see figure 27). What is said of them can be applied to other sites along this strand.

Wind-Sculpted Live Oaks at Salvo Campground

Just south of Salvo — a town named for an incident during the Civil War in which an unidentified Federal warship fired an unprovoked salvo at the collection of huts located here at the time — you can observe wonderful wind-sculpted live oaks at a National Park Service campground. The winds that shaped the trees came from both the northeast and the southwest, which makes these trees unique since most sculpted groves in this area were shaped by winds only from the northeast. Since northeast winds are the strongest, they are usually the most biologically significant. Although winds from the southwest are weaker, they are significant here because they strike the shoreface laden with salt picked up while crossing the 40 miles of Pamlico Sound. The live oak groves near the old graveyard at the northeast corner of the campground demonstrate the doubly-sculpted form especially well (see figure 28 and the cross section of this area in figure 27).

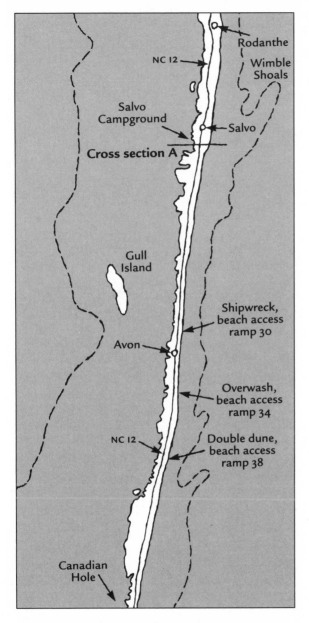

Figure 27. Rodanthe to Canadian Hole near Buxton. Base map from National Oceanic and Atmospheric Administration, National Ocean Service Chart 11555.

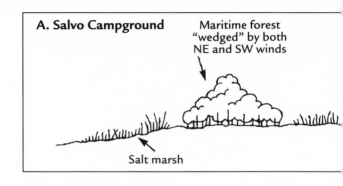

Figure 27.
Cross section.

Shipwrecks, Overwashes, and Dunes

Further south of Salvo, you will find examples of shipwrecks, overwashes, and palisade dunes. Three areas provide good parking, allowing easy access to these features.

Five miles south of Salvo (15.2 miles north of the Buxton post office), double dunes can be seen at beach access ramp 30. The remains of a wrecked wooden ship are located on the beach here. To examine another interesting site, travel 5.6 miles further south (10.6 miles south of Salvo; 9.6 miles north of the Buxton post office) to beach access ramp 34. Here the seaward (primary) dune has been destroyed by overwash, and the sand from it has been deposited on the original roadbed in front of the secondary dune. The road surface was demolished by the overwashing waves, as evidenced by the chunks of asphalt visible in the overwash fan (see figure 28). Note that the land within the overwash fan is higher than the land behind the primary dunes that remained intact. This is a good illustration of one way barrier islands gain elevation to keep up with rising sea level. Some of this sand finds its way onto the beach, creating areas of accreting rather than eroding shoreline.

The Little Kinnakeet Life-Saving Station is located about 9 miles south of Salvo (10 miles north of the Buxton post office). Note its attractive architecture and its placement far from the ocean and close to the ground.

One little-known fact about the Kinnakeet area is that the fans of athletic teams competing against Kinnakeet teams taunt the Kinnakeeters

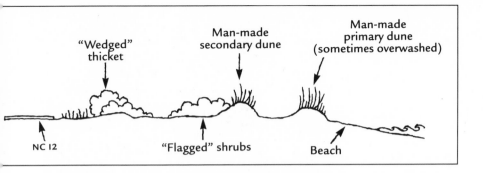

"Wedged" thicket

Man-made secondary dune

Man-made primary dune (sometimes overwashed)

NC 12

"Flagged" shrubs

Beach

with the infamous cheer: "Kinnakeeters, Kinnakeeters, they are all yaupon eaters." Eating yaupon, or, more commonly, drinking tea made from its leaves, is considered very déclassé on the Outer Banks. The high concentration of chemicals in the leaves causes vomiting—a quality that is recognized in yaupon's scientific name, *Ilex vomitoria*. In the 1800s, dried yaupon leaves were an important export from the Outer Banks, but the practice of purging one's digestive tract by drinking "spring tonics" disappeared around 1900, and the yaupon tea industry disappeared with it.

The third site is located another 5.2 miles south (15.8 miles south of Salvo; 4.4 miles north of the Buxton post office) at beach access ramp 38. Here the two palisade dunes remain intact, but the beginnings of an overwash can be detected on the primary dune just south of the beach access ramp. This dune has a cliff-like face on both its ocean side and the side near the access ramp. Such steep dune faces signal erosion by storm waves. If erosion continues, this area will begin to look more and more like the area at ramp 34. Closer inspection of the eroded dune faces reveals how subsurface plant materials protect the dune face from further erosion (see figure 12). Dune plants utilize a network of roots and rhizomes to collect rainwater as it drains rapidly through the dune sands. Here the network is exposed and hangs almost like a curtain across the recently eroded cliff face. The roots and rhizomes can remain alive for some time as long as they remain connected to living plants on the uneroded part of the dune. All parts of dune plants help keep incipient overwash from expanding.

A

Figure 28. High waves affect both sides of the Outer Banks.
(A) Wind-sculpted live oaks and graveyard at Salvo Campground. The gravestones were damaged by sound-side flooding during Hurricane Emily in 1993. Photograph by author.
(B) Overwash fan caused by ocean flooding at beach access ramp 34. Photograph by Watts Hill, Jr.
(C) The solution to overwash for beachfront houses is to make them "mobile" homes. Photograph by author.

Canadian Hole, a world-famous windsurfing venue south of Kinnakeet, is identifiable by its English-French sign (18.2 miles south of Salvo; 2 miles north of the Buxton post office). The waters on both sides of the Banks here are usually filled with windsurfers. The northeast and southwest winds of the Outer Banks are ideal for windsurfing because they blow across waves and surf on the windward side of the Banks and across a relatively wave-free sea on the leeward side. It is worth stopping here to see these colorful boards and their athletic sailors performing in a fresh breeze. The scene is an impressive example of a new and unexpected recreational potential of the Outer Banks utilized by an international subculture little known to most North Carolinians.

B

C

Hatteras Island

The elbow of Cape Hatteras is one of the most interesting areas on the Outer Banks. The cape itself is the main attraction; I urge visitors to spend some time here before moving to further explorations. Seven locations are worth visiting in this region: the site of Chacandepeco and New Buxton inlets, the Cape Hatteras Lighthouse, Buxton Woods Nature Trail, Cape Point, Hatteras Pines and Water Association Road, Frisco Campground dune area, and beach access areas near Hatteras Village (see figure 29).

Hatteras Island is 3.5 miles wide here, making it the widest barrier island between Kill Devil Hills and Wilmington. The width of the island supports a well-developed maritime forest known as Buxton Woods. Some geologists argue that this forest has helped Cape Hatteras resist erosion, causing it to retreat less than beaches to the north and south as sea level has risen over the last 17,000 years. This could explain both the unique offshore position of the cape and the more than right-angle shift in beach orientation. The habitats near Cape Hatteras demonstrate nearly the full range of habitats that can be found on the Outer Banks, and, except for the tip of Cape Point, they are easily accessible by automobile.

Chacandepeco and New Buxton Inlets

The historic site of both Chacandepeco and New Buxton inlets is located just south of Canadian Hole about 1.8 miles north of the Buxton post office. A parking area is available on the sound side of NC 12. Open before 1585, Chacandepeco Inlet was arguably the site where Francis Drake's shore party capsized in 1586 while trying to resupply Raleigh's colony on Roanoke Island. Chacandepeco Inlet closed in the 1650s; a shallow inlet called New Buxton opened at the same site in 1962 during a northeaster, only to be closed by a bulldozer shortly thereafter. The remains of the flood-tide delta of these inlets lie below the salt marsh islands directly west of the parking lot. Close examination of the water off of the sound shoreline reveals sandy shallows extending offshore to the marsh islands. These shallows are built of sand that was carried through the inlet when it opened. This area remains susceptible to inlet formation. In 1993 Hurricane Emily brought sound-side water within a few feet of overtopping the single dune line on the ocean side of the highway (see figure 30). Had this overtopping occurred, another New Buxton Inlet would probably have been formed in 1993. The possibility of such an occurrence is clear to anyone who climbs to the top of the dune line and sees the proximity of the ocean to the sound and the low and sandy land that separates them. The North Carolina Department of Transportation dredged sand from near Canadian Hole and added it to the beachface here in 1994 in an attempt to prevent inlet formation.

The dune at New Buxton Inlet is also a good place to view the Cape Hatteras Lighthouse to the south and the eastward-bulging beach in between (see figure 30). The reasons for the bulge will be apparent when you visit the lighthouse, where you can see up close the results of tampering with the sand transport system. Remember that somewhere between 500,000 and 1,000,000 cubic yards of sand are transported along this coast each year. Slow down that flow in one area, but not in another, and what would you expect to happen?

Cape Hatteras Lighthouse

At the time that the present Cape Hatteras Lighthouse was completed in 1870, it was located 1,500 feet from the ocean in the hopes that it would last at least 100 years. It has met this design criterion and, until 1936, served as the primary navigational beacon to help seafarers steer clear of Cape Hatteras and Diamond Shoals. Today the lighthouse has a new role as a national historic landmark, but its continued survival is threatened by a constantly advancing sea (see figure 31).

The formation of an eastward-bulging shoreline north of the lighthouse is a result of efforts to reduce beach erosion in front of the nearby U.S. Navy installation. Four steel and concrete walls (called groins by coastal engineers) have been constructed within the surf zone to slow sand transport along this stretch of beach. The good news is that sand is now stored in the beach north of the lighthouse; the bad news is the negative impact downstream, where erosion has increased dramatically. You

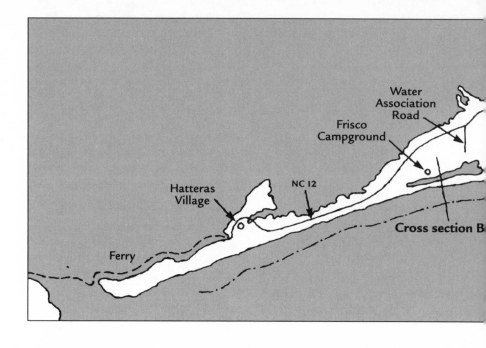

Water
Association
Road

Frisco
Campground

NC 12

Hatteras
Village

Cross section B

Ferry

don't have to be an "expert" to see the sharp 75-yard setback between the beach south of the lighthouse and the groin-stabilized beach to the north. The beach erosion rate south of the lighthouse increased from about 5 feet per year to over 12 feet per year during the adjustment period after the groins were built.

Despite the groins, the beach in front of the lighthouse has almost disappeared. Rocks, giant plastic sandbags, a man-made dune, and sand fences have been placed there in an attempt to reduce erosion. The severe beach erosion to the south proves that such structures merely shift erosion from one place to another; they do not stop it altogether. This lesson, learned so expensively in so many settings, has been incorporated into North Carolina's Coastal Area Management regulations, which prohibit the use of hard structures like rocks and groins to control beach erosion. Sometimes a perceived public interest causes the state to make exceptions to this sensible rule, as has occurred at Cape Hatteras Lighthouse. Fort

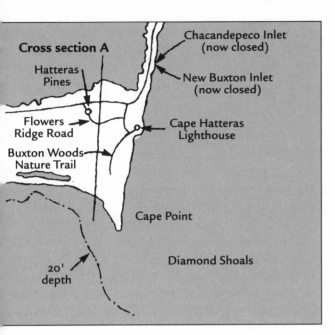

Figure 29. Hatteras Island. Base map from National Oceanic and Atmospheric Administration, National Ocean Service Chart 11555.

Fisher, a Civil War fort south of Wilmington that is also threatened by erosion, may become another example. Coastal-engineering structures do only what they are designed to do — protect small areas of beach from erosion. The consequences of instituting such protection measures can be assessed by anyone visiting the beaches near the Cape Hatteras Lighthouse.

Buxton Woods Nature Trail

The Buxton Woods Nature Trail is located just south of the entrance road from NC 12 to the lighthouse. This ¾-mile National Park Service trail makes a loop through a maritime forest situated between two freshwater ponds. The forest was badly damaged by Hurricane Emily in 1993, so visitors will see mostly forest recovery stages for the remainder of the twentieth century. The ridge and swale topography of the area consists of an alternating sequence of old dune ridges and interdune lows (swales); the

Figure 29.
Cross sections.

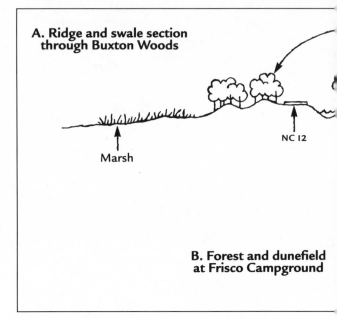

A. **Ridge and swale section through Buxton Woods**

Marsh

NC 12

B. **Forest and dunefield at Frisco Campground**

ridges now support maritime forests, and the interdune lows have become shallow ponds or freshwater swamps. The fact that these features alternate across the 3.5-mile width of Buxton Woods is viewed by geologists as a key to the history of this unusually wide part of the Outer Banks.

Coastal scientists base their explanation of the exceptional width of Hatteras Island upon the following observations:

1. Dunes form behind beaches when fine-grained sand is picked up by onshore winds and carried landward beyond the reach of waves and tides.

2. Some of the sand transported southward along the north-south beaches of Hatteras Island "turns the corner" and is deposited on the south-facing beach west of the cape, while the vast majority moves offshore to form Diamond Shoals.

3. This sand movement has changed the shape and position of Cape

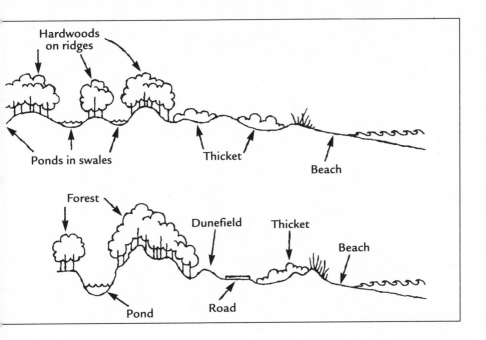

Hatteras, eroding the north/south beach westward and extending the east/west beach southward as new sand is added to it.

Figure 32 shows the changes in the position of Cape Hatteras from 1852 through 1965 that have resulted from these sand movements. The unusual width of the Buxton Woods section of Hatteras Island can be explained by all three observations. Dune ridges formed behind the south-facing beaches as sand was carried north by southwest winds (observation 1), and sand reaching the south-facing beach by "round the corner" alongshore transport (observation 2) continually added new dunes south of those formed earlier. As a result, the shore retreated to the west and extended southward (observation 3). The theory is given further support by the fact that the widest part of Buxton Woods is farthest east because sand blown from the east-facing beaches augments the sand supply of the eastern extremity of Buxton Woods.

A

   Buxton Woods Nature Trail is a good place to see evidence of the various sand transport processes and judge for yourself whether your observations support this theory. Begin the trail by climbing up a dune ridge that runs north to south, then turns to run east to west. Beyond this thought-provoking L-shaped ridge, the trail heads west along the south side of a shallow freshwater pond and marsh. These wetlands, called swales by botanists, seem to occupy an interdune low formed between two old primary dune ridges. Interpretive signs along the trail identify most of the common plants and animals that now occupy these ridges and swales. Hurricane Emily blew down many of the forest's oaks in 1993; pines may fill in the gaps as the forest recovers. Further along, the trail crosses a low sandy ridge and follows another swale running east to west, parallel to the first one. Beyond this second swale, you can see a much higher ridge topped by well-developed maritime forest and cottages that house park service employees. The trail loops back to complete its circuit

B

of ridge and swale topography with equal coverage of each — two ridges, two swales. Other ridge/swale units occur both north and south of the trail and can be observed from areas covered below. A schematic drawing of the topography of the Buxton Woods area of Hatteras Island is included in figure 29.

Cape Point

The beach access ramp to Cape Point heads south from a parking lot located just east of the Cape Point Campground. The ramp looks deceptively drivable from the parking lot because the section over a tall secondary dune has been stabilized with planks, but south of that dune, it passes through loose sand that is best traversed in a four-wheel-drive vehicle. I suggest leaving two-wheel-drive vehicles in the parking lot and

Figure 31. Cape Hatteras Lighthouse. Aerial photograph by author; close-up photograph by Watts Hill, Jr.

walking the 1.25 miles to Cape Point. It's a longish walk through soft sand, but it's worth it. Not only will you be able to stand at the exact point where the Outer Banks change directions, but you will also be able to observe several types of breaking waves and see sports fishermen and diving birds compete with each other for fish. Furthermore, upon your return, you will have some idea how Union and Confederate troops felt after they marched 24 miles along the Hatteras Island shore during the battle of Chicamacomico Races in 1862.

A typical dunefield thicket is located just south of the tall dune observable from the parking lot. The plants comprising the bulk of this thicket are groundsel, wax myrtle, yaupon holly, and sea elder. Beyond the thicket, the dunefield habitat continues in close proximity to a sand-bottomed pond that is usually filled with brackish water (less salty than the ocean; more salty than freshwater). Typical dune plants (dune spurge, sea oats, American beach grass, salt meadow cordgrass) occur in this area, along with very unusual species, including one — the sea beach amaranth (*Amaranthus pumilis*) — officially classified by the U.S. Fish and Wildlife Service as threatened with extinction. Terns and the threatened piping plover also nest on the dunes east of the pond. As a result, access to some areas is prohibited to prevent certain plants and nesting birds from being dis-

turbed. On the far side of the dunes, the access ramp (now only a track through soft sand) angles across the berm (the flat area behind the beach) to the beach itself.

The specific shape and features of the beach at Cape Point are impossible to predict because they change constantly due to the relatively high wave energy at this location. Most frequently, the east-facing beach is

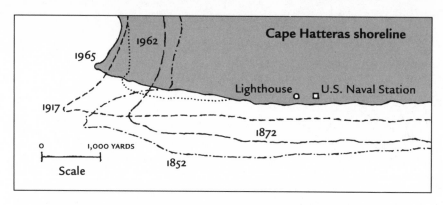

Figure 32. Shoreline changes at Cape Hatteras, 1852–1965. Redrawn from "The Outer Banks of North Carolina," U.S. Geological Survey Professional Paper 1177-B (1982), fig. 19, based on data from the U.S. Army Corps of Engineers.

steeper than the south-facing beach. Waves generally come from both the east and the south. As a result, most types of breakers and wave interactions can be seen in this area. All three types of breakers (plunging, spilling, and collapsing), described previously in Chapter 1, can usually be observed at Cape Point. Also, if it's warm enough to swim, you can use your body to measure the alongshore current by watching the beach as you float along toward Cape Point and the infamous Diamond Shoals beyond. The currents here can be strong, so be careful not to go too far from shore.

At the tip of Cape Point, you will see waves interacting with each other and with the seafloor. Interaction between waves can be positive, such as when two waves occupying the same spot create an unusually high crest as water from both waves is combined. Negative wave interaction occurs when one wave's crest occupies the area of another's trough so the two cancel each other out. The most dramatic wave interaction is called claptois and occurs when two crests moving in opposite directions slam into each other, causing water to spout violently into the air. Cape Point provides examples of claptois more frequently than any other place I know.

Wave interaction with the seafloor creates friction that slows the wave's forward motion and causes it to break. Friction between waves and the seafloor also causes waves to bend toward the beach as they approach, a process called refraction. This bending is easy to see at Cape Point because waves from the east bend around the point to break on the south-facing beach, and waves from the south bend around the point to break on the east-facing beach. In both cases, the portion of the wave crest closest to Cape Point slows in shallow water due to friction with the seafloor, while the portion further offshore continues at its original speed and moves ahead of, and thus around, the nearshore portion, thereby "bending" the wave crest so that it approaches the beach more or less head on.

Hatteras Pines and Water Association Road

Hatteras Island ranges in width from 3.5 miles at Buxton to something less than 1 mile at Frisco. The interior of this triangular area consists of ridges and swales similar to those seen along the Buxton Woods Nature Trail. This topography can be seen from a car at several other sites, but two are sufficiently illuminating to warrant mention here.

The first site can be reached by turning west from the entrance road to the lighthouse onto Flowers Ridge Road before you reach NC 12. Flowers Ridge Road continues about ½ mile to Buxton Back Road, west of the water tower. It can also be reached from Buxton Back Road by turning south onto Lost Tree Trail into Hatteras Pines. Lost Tree Trail crosses a water-filled swale, rises onto a ridge, then crosses another water-filled swale at the left turn onto Deer Run Trail. Deer Run Trail travels east on the south side of this second swale until it reaches what appears to be a cul-de-sac. A dirt road connects to the turnaround at its southeast corner, passes through an area of private homes, then eventually joins Flowers Ridge Road near the lighthouse entrance road.

The second area where ridge and swale topography can be seen by car is from Water Association Road, south of NC 12 about 2 miles west of the intersection of NC 12 and Buxton Back Road. The topography along Water Association Road is essentially similar to that in Hatteras Pines and along the Buxton Woods Nature Trail. The swales seen from Water Association Road are wider than those elsewhere, and the ridges are dominated more by pines than by live oaks, but the general sense of old dune ridges separated by water-filled interdune lows is the same. Water Association Road is open to the public as far as the water plant, but you must ask permission of Water Association employees at the plant before going further. Past the water plant, the road skirts the edge of the Water Association's well field, which provides freshwater from the "perched" water table that is exposed as ponds and swamps between the ridges. Such a water table occurs when freshwater from rainfall sinks rapidly through the sandy ridges, drains into the swales between the ridges, and then "perches" on top of salty groundwater that extends continuously from the ocean to the sound, deep under the island. It is worth arranging a trip to this area because the environments surrounding the well field have been left undeveloped to protect the purity of the water supply. As a result, the habitats here are those natural to Buxton Woods. Plans to convert part of this Water Association land into a nature preserve are worthy of support if the cost is not prohibitive.

Frisco Campground Dune Area

To reach Frisco Campground, turn onto Billy Mitchell Road, which intersects NC 12 about 3.5 miles west of Water Association Road almost directly across from the Frisco Native American Museum. Just before the entrance to the campground, paved parking areas are located on both sides of the road. South of the road, a well-marked trail leads to the beach. The trail traverses a fairly typical Outer Banks thicket. The dominant plants are groundsel, wax myrtle, sea elder, and yaupon holly.

North of the road, a well-developed dunefield with tall dunes fronts a maritime forest exhibiting the ridge and swale topography of the island interior (see figure 33). Climbing to the top of these dunes provides a spectacular view of South Beach, Cape Point, the Cape Hatteras Lighthouse, and the extensive dunefield in between. To the north, the land falls away to a water-filled swale about 60 feet below. A well-developed live oak forest occupies both the north-facing flank of the dune and the succession of parallel ridges north of it. The forest on the north face of the tallest dune was badly damaged by the winds of Hurricane Emily in 1993. A great deal of deadfall and the vines and thickets that are developing under new openings in the forest make walking difficult, but visitors who are dressed protectively (that is, those with boots, long pants, and long-sleeved shirts) may wish to work their way through the forest to gain insight into the damage a hurricane can do and an appreciation of the protection that a maritime forest affords dunes, even in hurricane-force winds.

Beach Access Areas near Hatteras Village

About 3 miles west of Frisco Campground, there are two beach access areas with boardwalks and parking, one of which has a public bathhouse. It is worth stopping at one of these areas to remind yourself how narrow the Outer Banks can be. At both sites, the island is less than ¹⁄₁₀ mile wide, and bulldozed sand testifies to the frequent occurrence of overwash events. The boardwalks at these sites make good vantage points from which to ponder the likelihood of the formation of new inlets across these narrow strands.

Another beach access and parking area is located southeast of NC 12 near the Hatteras/Ocracoke ferry dock. A stop here provides an opportunity to explore the westwardly elongating sand spit that extends almost 3 miles toward Ocracoke Island. The paved parking lot close to NC 12 is a good place to stop, or during damp weather, the sandy beach access road can be used even by two-wheel-drive vehicles. The road should be avoided if it is dry, however, because it is easy to get stuck here. (If you do get stuck, let some air out of your tires and proceed slowly; get a tow from a four-wheel-drive vehicle; or, if all else fails, call a tow truck.) The main beach access road is wide enough to provide parking, as are several grassy side roads. The extending spit that supports the road also supports a dense thicket community with a dunefield and beach on the ocean side and salt marsh on the sound side. The spit seems like a good place to escape the crowds of summertime beachgoers; those who travel to the end of it will find a good view of recent sand deposition along the east side of Hatteras Inlet. Beach accretion is mentioned much less than beach erosion in discussions of sand transport on barrier islands in the popular press. It does occur, however, and it is refreshing to see a place where sand is being deposited, such as here at the western end of Hatteras Island. But

Will Rogers was not wrong when he said, "Buy land son; they ain't making any more of it," for this land, although newly located here, was once beachfront somewhere else. Will was certainly right as far as barrier islands are concerned: they ain't making any more land on them.

Hatteras/Ocracoke Ferry across Hatteras Inlet

The Hatteras/Ocracoke ferry provides a 4-mile cruise across Hatteras Inlet. Hatteras Inlet opened in its present location in 1846 and gradually replaced Old Hatteras Inlet, located about 5 miles west. That inlet opened prior to 1657 but was always shallow and difficult to enter, so navigation and trade was concentrated around Ocracoke Inlet instead. The present Hatteras Inlet formed with a deep, navigable channel and rapidly became North Carolina's major trade and transshipment port from the 1850s through about 1900. Two forts were built to protect it during the Civil War, and their capture by Federal troops in 1862 resulted in the closing of North Carolina's sounds to trade for the duration of that conflict.

Hatteras Inlet is still more easily navigated than Ocracoke Inlet. As a result, a commercial/sportfishing port has developed in the town of Hatteras. The inlet continues to move, however. Ferry passengers can see evidence of the movement by noting the long sand spit extending west from the Hatteras Island ferry dock and the foundation pilings of an old Coast Guard station in the surf at the northeast end of Ocracoke. These features result from the migration of Hatteras Inlet toward the west. This migration occurs when sand carried by alongshore transport settles at the western end of Hatteras Island, forcing inlet currents to move further west, where they erode the eastern end of Ocracoke Island. Such erosion destroys whatever is "permanently" fixed there, such as the ill-fated Coast Guard station.

Ferry passengers can also see direct evidence of the movement of sand by tidal currents as the ferry follows its twisting course between the islands in order to insure safe passage through the shallow waters of the flood-tide delta. As tidal waters flood through the inlet, they carry sand into the sound, where it settles to form the flood-tide delta. The delta at

Hatteras Inlet is easily observed from the ferry—sometimes too easily observed, as ferries have been known to go aground on its constantly shifting lobes. A dredge is almost always working somewhere in the inlet, carrying on the never-ending battle to maintain an artificially deep channel in an area where sand is naturally deposited. Inlet dredging is one public works project that offers excellent job security.

The ebb-tide delta can usually also be seen on the trip across Hatteras Inlet. It is marked by breakers forming a semicircle across the mouth of the inlet from one side to the other. Observers seeing this ring of breakers can imagine the daunting prospect faced by early navigators as they contemplated "crossing the bar" into North Carolina's sounds. The inlets are still treacherous, even if the channels through them are now dredged and marked.

On the Hatteras Island side of the inlet, ferry passengers can see exposed shoals to the north of the channel. These shoals were formed as part of the flood-tide delta behind Hatteras Inlet before spit elongation moved it west to its present location. The sand in these shoals may be incorporated into Hatteras Island as it retreats landward as a result of rising sea level, as discussed in Chapter 1. Such incorporation of sand is one of the reasons why the Outer Banks vary in width from place to place.

From the Hatteras Island side of the channel, passengers can see a typically zoned salt marsh, with smooth cordgrass near the channel backed by black needlerush and thicket communities further into the spit. The edge of this marsh is eroding in many places, perhaps because of rising sea level but more likely in response to the large and numerous boat wakes that pound this shoreline.

Ocracoke Island

Ocracoke Island extends for about 18 miles from Hatteras Inlet to Ocracoke Inlet. The town of Ocracoke—a major ocean port and transshipment site during the American Revolution—is located at the southwestern end on the widest point of the island as far from the ocean as possible. Nearly the entire island is in the hands of the National Park Service, which, with the help of the U.S. Army Corps of Engineers, "stabilized" it in the mid-1960s by building two palisade dunes along the ocean side. These dunes have blocked overwash events for almost 20 years and thereby encouraged the rapid development of thickets and of pine-dominated maritime forests. Now these artificial dunes have been breached by overwash in several places, particularly along the northeastern third of the island. These overwashes are making the island higher but periodically cover NC 12 with sand.

Four locations on Ocracoke Island illustrate the range of natural areas to be found here: the overwash area between the ferry dock and the Ocracoke Island Pony Pen; Parker's Creek dunefield and thicket; Hammock Hills Nature Trail; and Blackbeard's camp (see figure 33).

Overwash Area between the Ferry Dock
and the Ocracoke Island Pony Pen

Dune overwash areas occur almost anywhere along the northeastern third of the island, but the most convenient area to explore is located near a parking spot about 3.2 miles west of the Hatteras/Ocracoke ferry dock (10.8 miles east of the Ocracoke post office). Visitors should note two things here: the overwash fans, delta-like fans of sand extending back from low points between the taller primary dunes, and examples of various dune-rebuilding efforts, ranging from sand bulldozed into the interdune lows and replanted with sprigs of American beach grass (a species that rarely occurs naturally south of Cape Hatteras) to sandbagged and bulldozed artificial dunes protecting the ocean side of NC 12 (see figure 33 for a cross section).

It is important to remember that overwash is a natural process that widens and heightens the island and that species of dune plants and animals are well adapted to it. Plant ecologists believe that overwash has been a regular feature of Outer Banks ecology for thousands of years. It has contributed to the island's survival during the present period of rising sea level and has maintained the biological diversity of island communities by providing new sand surfaces for colonization by the plants that stabilize such surfaces against continued movement by winds.

Overwash events in this area of Ocracoke Island precipitated an interesting and controversial dune restoration effort in 1994. About 4 miles of NC 12 were overwashed by high waves and tides caused by Hurricane Gordon in November. Sand from the beach and dunes was deposited on the highway to depths of several feet. The established procedure in such cases is for the matter to be resolved by the NC 12 Task Force — a group of public officials representing state and federal agencies involved in Outer Banks transportation and environmental affairs. This group has been able to devise practical and environmentally acceptable plans for clearing and protecting NC 12 but, for some reason, was not asked to do so in this area in 1994. Instead, the North Carolina Department of Transportation acted unilaterally and bulldozed more than 30 acres of natural dune area, much of it outside the highway right-of-way, to construct the steep-sided artificial dune shown in figure 34. This solution proved unacceptable to the National Park Service and exceeded the authority granted the department by the North Carolina Office of Coastal Management. Subsequent interagency negotiations have resulted in an agreement that the Department of Transportation reshape the front of the new dune to produce a more gradual and natural slope toward the beach, restore the backdune area to its previous level (more than 2 feet of sand was removed in many areas), and plant native dune plants on the restored backdune surface. The Department of Transportation received a notice of permit violation and a fine for its precipitate and environmentally insensitive handling of the Hurricane Gordon overwash.

The Ocracoke Island Pony Pen is located about 6.6 miles west of the Hatteras/Ocracoke ferry dock (7.4 miles east of the Ocracoke post office). The park service has built a raised platform to make it easier for visitors to observe the ponies. These ponies, like those in Corolla, show significant genetic similarities to Spanish horses. The idea that Outer Banks horses might actually have descended from equine survivors of Spanish shipwrecks adds romance and interest to these animals. Whatever the origin of the ponies, however, their grazing has an adverse effect on sediment-stabilizing dune and marsh plants. Note the close-cropped grass within the pony pen compared to the much taller grasses of the nearby dunes and marshes. These shorter grasses provide less protection for the sand

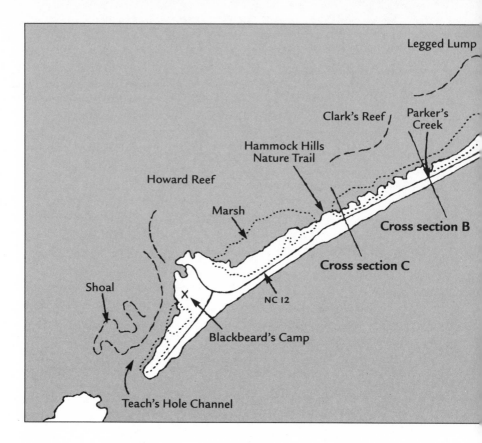

beneath them as they cause less turbulence in the windfield than taller plants do.

Parker's Creek Dunefield and Thicket

Parker's Creek is located about 7.4 miles west of the Hatteras/Ocracoke ferry dock (6.6 miles east of the Ocracoke post office). The ground along the roadside here is hard enough for parking (that's not the basis for the creek's name, however). The sandy trail that leads to the beach passes through wedged thickets of wax myrtle, yaupon holly, groundsel, and

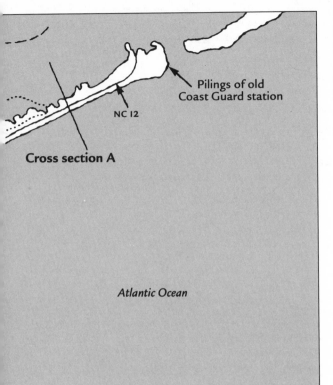

Figure 33. Ocracoke Island. Base map from National Oceanic and Atmospheric Administration, National Ocean Service Chart 11555.

Pilings of old
Coast Guard station

NC 12

Cross section A

Atlantic Ocean

Spanish bayonet. The trail crosses a dunefield characterized by American beach grass, salt meadow cordgrass, sea oats, southern bayberry, prickly pear cactus, horseweed, dune spurge, and pennywort. This is as diverse an assemblage of dune plants as occurs anywhere on Ocracoke (see figure 33 for a cross section). The trail also passes near the partial remains of a wrecked sailing ship. The remains provide enough shelter for southern bayberry to flourish where it otherwise would not. The trail ends after winding up and over the artificial secondary and primary dunes behind the beach. Careful observers will note that sea oats grow at the tops of these dunes and at other exposed locations throughout the dunefield.

Figure 33.
Cross sections.

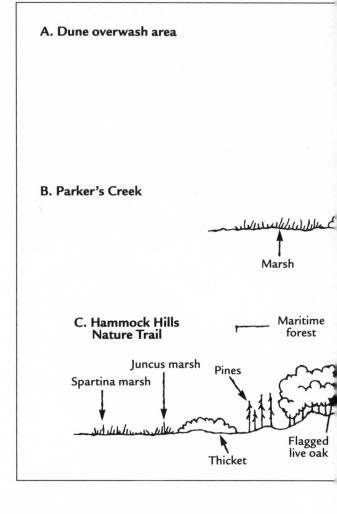

A. Dune overwash area

B. Parker's Creek

Marsh

C. Hammock Hills
Nature Trail

Maritime forest

Juncus marsh

Spartina marsh

Pines

Thicket

Flagged live oak

This plant differs from the others in that it has a greater tolerance for salt spray. The front of the primary dune here is often cliff-like as a result of erosion by storm waves. If that is the case at the time of your visit, note the network of roots and sea oat remnants that cover the cliff face.

On the sound side of NC 12 at Parker's Creek is a well-developed, almost

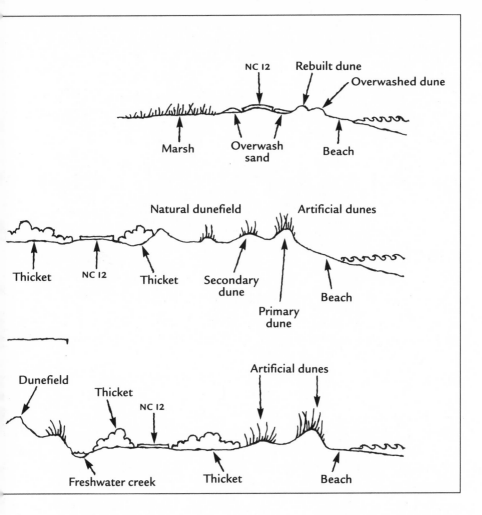

impenetrable thicket. You can get some idea of the density of this community by observing it from the highway bridge over the creek or from paths beside the creek.

Figure 34. Environmentally unacceptable overwash repair on Ocracoke Island in 1995. Photographs by author.

Hammock Hills Nature Trail

About 10 miles west of the Hatteras/Ocracoke ferry dock (4 miles east of the Ocracoke post office), you will find the parking area for the Hammock Hills Nature Trail on the north side of NC 12. The lot is about 100 yards west of the Ocracoke Campground entrance. This well-planned trail is arranged so that you enter new habitat types after rounding a corner, thus emphasizing differences between adjacent habitats and delighting the senses with surprising new vistas around each bend. Even if your time is limited, you should visit this trail. Be sure to wear old or waterproof shoes and bring binoculars to view the abundant bird life. The trail is about ¾ of a mile long and winds around among thicket, dune, maritime forest, and salt marsh habitats (see figure 33 for a cross section).

After entering the trail underneath a power line, turn left into a typical

Outer Banks thicket. A marker identifies three of the dominant thicket shrubs here: groundsel, wax myrtle, and yaupon holly. Other shrubs in the thickets include small red cedars, Spanish bayonet, and sea elder. Sea elder is a fleshy-leaved shrub of the aster family with leaves located on alternate sides of the stem. It is otherwise very similar to the marsh elder, whose leaves are opposite each other at the same point on the stem. (You'll see marsh elder further along the trail, when you get to the marsh-bordered thicket on the sound side of the island.)

Within this thicket, but bordered by marsh plants, is a freshwater creek much used by wading and diving birds. The presence of standing freshwater within thicket and maritime forest habitats of the Outer Banks is tangible evidence of a perched water table. Perched water tables are exposed in creeks and mid-island ponds throughout Ocracoke and elsewhere along the Outer Banks.

After crossing the creek, the trail veers left into a stand of young slash pines that was planted here in the 1950s. Note the very large specimens of black needlerush that grow beneath the pines. This rush is usually found along the upland edge of salt marshes. The fact that it grows vigorously under these pines suggests that its occurrence in many freshwater habitats may be hampered by competition with grasses or other marsh plants better adapted to open settings. Note also the infrequency of pine seedlings under the medium-size pines of the forest. Pine trees are victims of their own success in that their dense stands create a shady forest floor upon which their own seeds cannot germinate and grow. As a result, pine forests are only a stage in an ecological succession during which one group of plants and animals replaces another until a self-reproducing "climax community" is established. In Outer Banks maritime forests, the most frequent "climax community" is one dominated by live oaks. The pine stand along Hammock Hills Nature Trail is in the process of being replaced by hardwoods. Saplings of marsh magnolia and other hardwoods already established beneath the pine overstory (the top layer of a forest canopy) are evidence that this process is taking place.

After the trail leaves the pine forest, it enters a dunefield that contains some pines as well as somewhat more typical dune plants, such as prickly pear cactus, Spanish bayonet, and several vines (catbrier or greenbrier, Virginia creeper, and pepper vine). The most typical of all exposed dune plants — sea oats — occupies the dune crest, which offers an ocean view. Behind the dune crest, you can see a salt-spray-stunted live oak, the first of its species to establish itself in this habitat.

The trail leaves the dunefield by skirting a low and well-vegetated dune, then plunges into a mature pine forest with a distinctly developed understory of hardwoods — mostly marsh magnolia, myrtles, and young live oaks. After passing through the forest, the trail enters the sound-side thicket and salt marsh. Many of the plants here are the same as those found elsewhere along the trail, but marsh elder is now more abundant than sea elder and black needlerush is more stunted than it was near the freshwater creek. The marsh itself is typically zoned, with thicket grading to black needlerush and needlerush grading to salt marsh cordgrass near the water. The park service signposts describe the crabs (fiddlers and squarebacks) that occupy the marsh as well as some of the small vertebrates (raccoons, rabbits, and rice rats) that live in marsh and thicket habitats. Wading birds and other waterfowl are often seen in the marsh-bordered embayment north of the boardwalk. The nearshore shallows extend northward for more than a mile before the sound gets deeper on the far side of Clark's Reef, sometimes discernible as a line of breakers a mile or more offshore.

The trail continues to the right, beyond a boardwalk through a stand of young pines, where it traverses an extensive dunefield. A variety of dune habitats can be seen from the trail; it also affords a good view of marsh "hammocks" located between this point and Ocracoke village. These forested hammocks are slightly higher and sandier than the surrounding marsh and may represent old dune ridges at what was once the western end of Ocracoke.

From the parking lot, you can walk the rest of the way across the island by crossing NC 12 and continuing eastward along a beach access road. The thicket habitat along the access road contains plants similar to those found along the nature trail, as does the dunefield beyond. Note the low oceanside edge of the thicket and the severely flagged shrubs within the dunefield. Both are examples of how salt spray sculpts plants into a shape that reduces exposure to salt-laden ocean winds.

Blackbeard's Camp

For a view of the forested area where Edward Teach, the infamous Blackbeard the Pirate, is thought to have made camp, take the sandy beach road that joins NC 12 just west of Ocracoke Airport about 14 miles west of the Hatteras/Ocracoke ferry dock (1/10 mile east of the Ocracoke post office). It is passable in a two-wheel-drive car except during extended dry spells but probably should be avoided if loose, dry sand is deeply piled on its surface. About 1.5 miles down the beach road, another road to the right leads about 1/4 mile to the banks of Teach's Hole Channel. West of here, you can see the maritime forest where Blackbeard possibly camped in 1718. The environmental features observable from this spot include the typically zoned salt marsh, with thicket, needlerush, and smooth cord-grass areas in sequence from high ground to the water's edge, and the salt spray sculpted edge of the forest in the distance.

Conclusion

A trip along the Outer Banks demonstrates the diversity of landscapes that result from different interactions between wind, water, sand, and plants. At one topographic extreme lies the almost mountainous Jockey's Ridge; at the other, areas scrubbed flat by overwash events. Botanically, the forest at Nags Head Woods is as complex as any on the coastal plain, but within a few hundred feet, single species stands of dune grass hold tenuously to existence at the peak of Run Hill. The most interesting aspect of these observations is that they can be explained within a fairly simple context of environmental processes. The rise of sea level produces landward movement of barrier islands, which is carried out by dune migration, overwash events, and the incorporation of flood-tide delta deposits behind inlets. All of these sand and island movements are initiated by wind and the energy of waves breaking on the shoreface. Plants are the only natural features that slow this movement and hold sand grains in place. Human habitation on these landforms cannot be viewed as permanent because the land must eventually move out from under whatever is built upon it. These observations are clearly simplifications, but, if extended, they provide a good approximation of the nature of the Outer Banks and the implications of these natural systems for human habitation upon them.

CHAPTER THREE

ISSUES FOR THE FUTURE

The issues that affect the future of the Outer Banks grow out of the unique environment of the Banks. The Banks are isolated, dynamic, and finite, a place where natural resources set limits to growth and development.

Natural scientists spend much of their time studying problems of resource abundance. Geologists assess the presence of natural resources such as oil, minerals, precious metals, and gemstones in the scientific context of the earth's history; they try to understand how the earth came to be the way it is today in the hopes that such knowledge will help them locate developable resources. Guided by the principle, "The present is the key to the past," they study geologic processes occurring today to help them understand how geologic resources were formed in the past. To assess Banks resources, we must understand both the geology and ecology of the Banks. Much of Chapters 1 and 2 describes how environmental processes have shaped Banks landforms and plant life. But natural scientists' resource development scenarios must use the present not only as a key to the past but also as a key to the future. In a sense, this approach reframes the geologist's motto in light of the historian's cautionary adage: "Those who do not know history are destined to repeat it."

History of Outer Banks Resource Use

The history of Outer Banks resource development began in the colonial era. Natural scientists divide it into three phases: a subsistence phase, during which development was controlled by the local resource base and by characteristics of the natural environment; a transitional phase, during which the subsistence economy was supplemented by nonlocal resources and humans began to modify, if not understand, characteristics of the natural environment; and a modern phase, during which humans have become largely dependent on nonlocal resources but with development modifications increasingly based on an understanding of the natural environment. Placing actual Outer Banks history within this framework suggests that the first phase took place from the colonial era up to about the Civil War, the second phase took place from the Civil War to the 1950s, and the third phase is occurring now. The subsistence phase has been described extensively elsewhere. So as to avoid the consequences of not heeding the historian's adage, however, we will briefly review the history of Outer Banks resource use in the transitional and modern phases to gain insights that might be useful in our consideration of the future. We will then focus on fisheries as an example of resource development constrained by finite resources and consider water supply and wastewater disposal as examples of development essentials that control the size of sustainable human populations.

Two major themes underlie Outer Banks development since the Civil War: public investment in infrastructure and private enterprise built upon that infrastructure. Since that time, public investment to support commerce and coastal development has continued to increase — first with ports, pilots, lighthouses, and life-saving stations to support private enterprise in the maritime trades; next with weather and coastal research stations established to study the Banks environment; and finally with development infrastructure built to provide roads, protective dunes, water supplies, and waste disposal facilities. These projects fundamentally changed the nature of the Banks and the density of human populations that could live there.

Economic development of Banks resources began slowly but accelerated rapidly in the mid-twentieth century. At the time of the Civil War, according to 1860 census data, only about 1,200 people and 200 dwellings existed on all of Hatteras Island. Ninety years later, the value of Outer Banks real estate in Dare County was assessed at about $6 million. The growth in assessed value since then is summarized in table 1. It is clear that public investment in infrastructure has provided ample opportunity for private enterprise to develop on the Outer Banks. Today's Outer Bankers are a far cry from those characterized as "wild people" by an eighteenth-century magistrate and as "queer folks . . . who get their living by fishing, gathering oysters, wrecking and piloting" by a mid-nineteenth-century observer. A more thoughtful early assessment was made by a Confederate officer who David Stick in *The Outer Banks of North Carolina* (1958) quotes as saying: "The islanders mingle but little with the world. Apparently indifferent to this outside sphere, they constitute a world within themselves" (p. 154). The change from existing as a "world within themselves" to being the worldly-wise property owners of today began in the decades immediately after the Civil War.

The Outer Banks figured only briefly in the Civil War, but the impact of Federal occupation and the postwar importance of the Banks to coastwise trade forced the Bankers to give up their splendid isolation in the latter part of the nineteenth century. Federal investment in lighthouses and life-saving stations paved the way into the modern world. Increasing trade along the Atlantic coast made the dangers of nearshore navigation along the Banks a national crisis. A quick look at figure 35 shows why. A ship leaving deepwater northern ports for the south had to sail seaward around Cape Hatteras and its offshore extension, Diamond Shoals. If the ship strayed too far offshore, it had to stem the 4- to 6-mile-per-hour current of the Gulf Stream. As a result, most ships stayed inshore, risking the shallows. Rounding Cape Hatteras and its shoals was made even more difficult when winds and currents came from the southwest, as was most often the case. Rounding Cape Hatteras in a sailing ship was so difficult that, even early in this century, more than 100 ships at a time might collect north of the cape as they tacked back and forth, waiting for a favorable shift in wind or current.

The problem was not new, but its importance grew as the volume of

Table 1. Assessed Value of Outer Banks Real Estate in Dare County, 1950–93

	Total Assessed Value
1950	$5.986 million
1960	$18.012 million
1970	$34.036 million
1981	$311.345 million
1993	$3,510.843 million

Source: Data from Dare County Tax Assessor's Office, 1994.

trade increased. Early lighthouses built to assist mariners navigating along the Banks were hopelessly inadequate to the needs of the mid-1800s. The first lighthouse at Hatteras was described as "a disgrace to our country," and one coastal captain advised that all lights in North Carolina "if not improved, had better be dispensed with, as the navigator is apt to run ashore looking for them." These complaints prompted action from the U.S. Light House Board, which built a new 150-foot brick lighthouse at Cape Lookout in 1857–59 and made plans to build others along the Banks. The Civil War interrupted those plans, but Congress appropriated $75,000 for the construction of a new 180-foot brick-on-granite lighthouse at Cape Hatteras in 1867.

Completed in 1870, the Cape Hatteras Lighthouse was designed to last 100 years. The Light House Board decreed that "this structure shall be of as durable a character as the nature of the materials . . . will admit." Its foundation was made of two courses of 6-by-9-inch yellow pine timbers laid crosswise to each other, 6 feet below the sand—a depth where they would be protected from rotting by being underwater. The granite blocks that can be seen today were then laid atop these timbers. The design, materials, and construction have more than met the board's criteria. After the recent renovation of the metal staircase, the lighthouse is as sound today as it was well over a century ago; the only problem is that erosion now threatens its foundation. A panel from the National Academy of Sciences has examined the problem and determined that it would be possi-

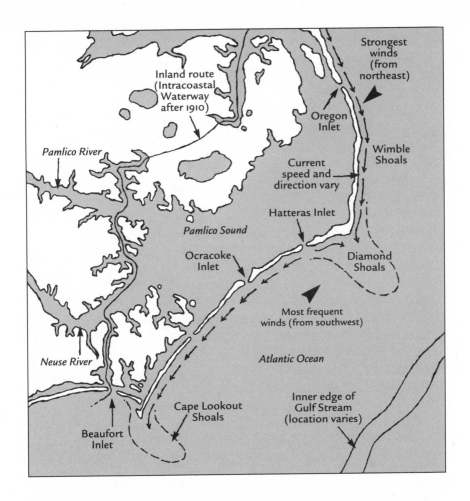

Figure 35. Currents, winds, and shoals off the Outer Banks. Navigation hazards off the Outer Banks resulted from strong currents, adverse winds, and offshore shoals. The Gulf Stream slowed southbound ships sailing offshore, forcing them near the shore and shoals. Winds from the southwest made rounding the capes difficult. Nearshore currents slowed northbound ships, and strong winds from northeasters made rounding the capes nearly impossible. As a result, an alternate navigation route, the Intracoastal Waterway, was developed early in the twentieth century. Base map from North Carolina Department of Transportation.

ble to move the lighthouse. Plans for such a move have been made, and when funding is available, the Cape Hatteras Lighthouse will be moved back from the sea to survive into future centuries.

Other lighthouses followed. Once the design, logistics, and construction crews were in place, lighting the "Graveyard of the Atlantic" became only a matter of money. The new Bodie Island Lighthouse was completed in 1872, and the Currituck Beach Lighthouse was completed at Corolla in 1875. These projects provided the first steady employment for the Bankers but did not entirely eliminate shipwrecks along the shore. David Stick in *Graveyard of the Atlantic* (pp. 244–57) lists 393 ships known to have wrecked along the Outer Banks between 1526 and 1940 (see table 2).

The many lives lost in shipwrecks along the Banks led directly to another federal program to assist the maritime trade — the creation of a network of life-saving stations. Seven U.S. Life-Saving Service stations were built along the Outer Banks in 1874. These stations were located at least 15 miles apart, had a complement of only seven men each (one keeper, six surf men), and operated only during the four winter months. The loss of almost 200 lives in the wrecks of the *Huron* and the *Metropolis* in the late 1870s spurred expansion of the network. By 1879, 11 new stations were in operation, and another 8 were added later to bring the total to 26. By 1883, these stations were operating eight months each year. Details of the heroic exploits of the life-saving crews are provided by David Stick in *Graveyard of the Atlantic* and by Nell Wise Wechter in *The Mighty Midgetts of Chicamacomico*.

The U.S. Life-Saving Service quickly became the major employer on the Banks. By 1883, at least 182 people were working at the stations — a substantial number in a population of about 1,500. Stick in *The Outer Banks of North Carolina* (p. 176) cites statistics from the 1950 census of Dare County stating that 93 of the 179 heads of families in Avon, Rodanthe, Waves, and Salvo were either retired from (56) or active in (37) the U.S. Coast Guard — the agency formed in 1915 by combining the U.S. Life-Saving Service with the Revenue Cutter Service. Regular income from this and other federal employment brought a cash economy to the Outer Banks and did much to initiate private development of the Banks.

Other government agencies employed Bankers. The U.S. Weather Ser-

Table 2. Shipwrecks along the Outer Banks, 1526–1939

	Number of Wrecks	Known Lives Lost
1526–1839	40	133 (90 in 1837, schooner *Howe*)
1840–59	68	38 (11 in 1854, *Robert Walsh*)
1860–79	70	253 (98 in 1877, steamer *Huron*)
		(85 in 1878, steamer *Metropolis*)
1880–99	113	124 (40 in two wrecks)
1900–1919	75	167 (49 in 1915, steamer *Prince Maurits*)
1920–39	27	53 (25 in 1924, steamer *Santiago*)

Source: Data from David Stick, *Graveyard of the Atlantic: Shipwrecks of the North Carolina Coast* (Chapel Hill: University of North Carolina Press, 1952), pp. 244–57.

vice established a station at Cape Hatteras in 1874 and another at Kitty Hawk in 1875. The U.S. Postal Service installed a total of seventeen new post offices between Cape Lookout and the Virginia border between 1765 and 1910. The post offices changed both the lexicon and the economy of the Outer Banks forever. Place names changed as applicants for post offices, and the officials who approved them, rejected names that were too long or hard to spell and substituted names of their own choosing. Thus Kinnakeet became Avon, the Cape became Buxton, Roanoke Island briefly became Skyco, Whales Head/Currituck Beach became Corolla, Trent became Frisco, Clarks became Salvo, and Wash Woods became Deals.

The loss of some of the old, familiar names was partially offset by the greater ease of communication with the outside world and the impetus for development provided by the expanded service. Not only could Bankers send and receive mail on a regular basis, but non-Bankers could write to the postmaster seeking advice on trips to the Banks, sources for Outer Banks goods they wished to buy, means of access to the Banks, and the like. The late nineteenth-century postmaster performed many of the functions of today's Chambers of Commerce. The most famous and far-reaching example was Postmaster Will Tate's response to a letter written to the U.S. Weather Service in Kitty Hawk by a young bicycle shop owner in Ohio—one Wilbur Wright. Tate answered Wright's questions about local winds and whether open ground suitable for experiments with a flying machine was available, provided explicit directions on how to reach Kitty Hawk, gave advice concerning the times of year most suitable for kite flying, and offered to help Wilbur and his brother Orville achieve success in their efforts to build a flying machine. Never has a dose of southern hospitality had a more revolutionary impact on the world than did William Tate's 1900 letter to the Wright brothers.

Federal construction projects outside the Banks also had a profound impact on the Banks' economy and development. The continued loss of ships and lives in coastwise trade in the late 1800s, coupled with increased siltation in Ocracoke and Hatteras inlets, led to the creation of an inland route from Chesapeake Bay south. The commercial traffic through the Albemarle and Chesapeake Canal increased during the early 1900s. The federal government purchased a private canal connecting Pamlico Sound with Beaufort in 1913 and replaced the open route from Albemarle Sound to Pamlico Sound with a canal connecting the Alligator River to the Pungo River. In this way, an inland canal 10 feet deep between Chesapeake Bay and Beaufort was established (see figure 35). This route, along with its extensions north and south, is now known as the Intracoastal Waterway. According to David Stick in *The Outer Banks of North Carolina*, the creation of this inland waterway ended "the days of extensive maritime activity along the Banks" (p. 183).

Profitable private enterprise followed the establishment of federal infrastructure on the Banks. Convenient steamer service to mid-Atlantic cities across Albemarle Sound greatly expanded trade and tourism, which led to economic development. The first to feel the impact were fish and shellfish. Surprisingly enough, fishing was not a major occupation of Outer Bankers before the late nineteenth century. In the 1850 census of Ocracoke and Portsmouth, fewer than 7 percent of the heads of households listed their occupation as fisherman. The small percentage of fishermen is easier to understand if one remembers how isolated the Banks were at that time and how rapidly most fish spoil. Anyone who has tried to give fish to friends knows that a large catch can be a liability rather than an asset if you can't find enough people to take them or have no convenient way to preserve them. As a result of the lack of preservation methods and transportation, most Bankers caught only the amount of fish they needed for their families. The economic significance of fish changed completely once reliable transportation to northern markets was available. Private enterprise rushed in to exploit the change.

The earliest commercial fisheries focused on fish like mullet, herring, and shad, which could be preserved by smoking or salting. By the 1870s, millions of pounds of salted mullet were shipped out each year. Within a decade, shad and herring were also being caught in great quantities, and the large-scale harvest of oysters had begun. The extent of these catches began to cause problems, however. First came conflicts about fishing rights. As early as 1891, North Carolinians were seeking state assistance in preventing Chesapeake dredgers from harvesting local oysters; and overharvest, disease, and diminished water quality were contributing to a steady decline of this fishery by 1903. Figure 36 summarizes the trend in annual oyster harvest and identifies some of the reasons why the harvest rate has declined throughout the twentieth century.

The decline of another natural resource, migratory waterfowl, requires no such complex explanation. Like fishing, hunting was practiced by almost all Bankers, but very few earned their living from it before the late 1800s. As with fisheries, private enterprise took advantage of late nineteenth-century access to markets and developed a new trade — commercial hunting from boats or from "sink boxes" (wooden boxes placed in shallow water from which hunters shot waterfowl at eye level). Guns evolved from muzzle loaders to double-barreled, then automatic, shotguns. Some hunters even used cannon-like devices mounted on small boats called punt guns. Dead birds were sold, iced, and shipped north to market. Prices ranged from 25 cents to $2.00 per bird, with canvasback and redhead ducks being most valuable. In 1905 two Currituck Sound gunners established a local record when they killed 892 ruddy ducks in a single day. Not surprisingly, this level of slaughter in North Carolina and elsewhere along the migration routes decreased the size of the flocks tremendously. Wealthy sports hunters became concerned, and in 1918 Congress outlawed commercial hunting by passing the Migratory Bird Treaty Act.

As is clear to all observers, the modern economy of the Outer Banks is

Figure 36. North Carolina oyster harvest, 1887–1994. The natural stock of oysters provided large but unsustainable harvests into the early 1900s. Increased dredging efficiency, hurricanes, and the harvest of prereproductive individuals caused harvests to decline. Regrowth during World War I was eliminated by expanded dredging and storms. Regrowth during World War II lasted almost 20 years due to harvest restrictions, but disease, storms, and Hurricane Ginger brought the harvest to current low levels by 1970. Oyster rehabilitation and management seemed to improve fishery conditions into the late 1980s, but another disease outbreak and environmentally degraded shellfish beds brought harvests to historically low levels in the mid-1990s. Modified from North Carolina Division of Marine Fisheries, "North Carolina Oyster Management Plan," fig. 3, p. 20.

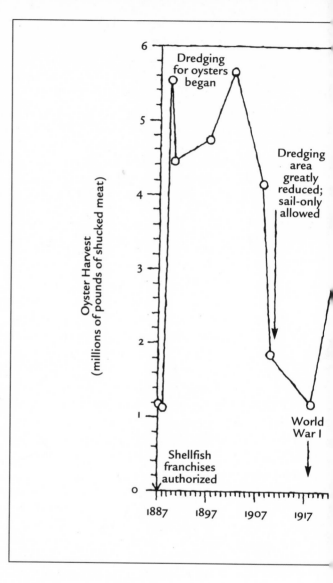

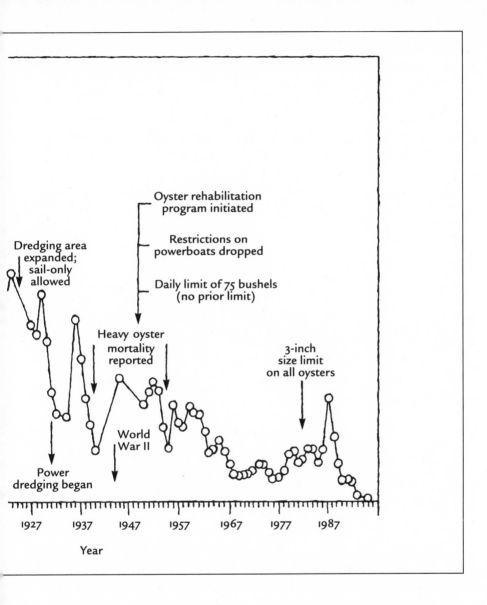

Dredging area expanded; sail-only allowed

Oyster rehabilitation program initiated

Restrictions on powerboats dropped

Daily limit of 75 bushels (no prior limit)

Heavy oyster mortality reported

3-inch size limit on all oysters

World War II

Power dredging began

1927   1937   1947   1957   1967   1977   1987

Year

driven by tourism and recreation, not commercial hunting or fishing. The recreation business got its start in the 1830s, when planters and merchants began to summer in Nags Head to escape the heat and malaria of the coastal plain. By late in the decade, a hotel with a large ballroom supplemented the summer cottages on the sound side of Nags Head; another was opened by 1841. By the mid-1850s, Nags Head was featured in articles in *Harpers New Monthly Magazine* that described a well-developed social life. Naturally, the development of a tourist industry came to a screeching halt during the Civil War, when the retreating Confederates burned the hotels. But by 1867, summer tourism in Nags Head was back in business. Interestingly enough, development was limited to the sound side until the mid-1880s. The summer community well understood that they had only a tenuous grasp on the shifting sands of the Banks. Several hotels went out of business after migrating dunes covered them in the 1880s, just as a 1980s Putt-Putt Golf Course closed after being buried by sands from Jockey's Ridge. Beachfront residences were first built in 1884, and many of the early cottages are among the houses known today as the "unpainted aristocracy" near Soundside Road in Nags Head (see Chapter 2). Books such as Catherine Bishir's *The "Unpainted Aristocracy": The Beach Cottages of Old Nags Head* (1977) explain the nostalgia that three generations of North Carolinians feel for the Outer Banks era of pony carts, boardwalks, and long summer house parties.

The small summer resort at Nags Head could not sustain the economy of the Banks alone, however. By the 1920s, shipbuilding, whaling, and commercial hunting had stopped completely, and commercial fishing had become less profitable as a result of overharvest and the near extinction of some of the most valuable species (whales, sea turtles, sturgeon, diamondback terrapins). Overgrazing by cattle, sheep, and goats had denuded the dunes, so active dunes shifted across the Banks in response to the winds. Several Banks communities (Diamond City, Little Kinnakeet) had been abandoned, and others (Portsmouth, Ocracoke, Hatteras) were at risk. The summer resort at Nags Head was profitable, but isolation restricted its growth. The 1920s economy of the Banks was a shambles. Washington Baum, the newly elected mayor of Manteo, decided to do something to stimulate the economy.

Mayor Baum realized that measures taken in Dare County, the home of 80 percent of Banks residents, would affect the future of the entire Outer Banks. Dare County was important to the Banks, both politically and economically, but it was also isolated and internally divided. The different parts of the county were not connected to each other by roads, much less to the mainland cities from which visitors might come. The beaches were clearly an asset but could be reached only by boat and pony cart, whereas the rest of the United States had entered the era of the automobile. Washington Baum set out to obtain funding to build roads and bridges. Rebuffed by the state in his efforts to connect Dare's beaches to the mainland, Baum secured permission to sell bonds to finance the construction of the first causeway and bridge connecting Manteo to Nags Head in 1927. Needless to say, many Dare Countians thought Baum's bridge was the local equivalent of Seward's Folly, but the $1.00 toll began to pay off the bonds, and people skilled at driving on the sand could travel up and down the Banks.

Most important, the success of the Roanoke Sound bridge led to the construction of a bridge across Currituck Sound north of Kitty Hawk. Built by developers to encourage sales of land they owned, the bridge was named the Wright Brothers Memorial Bridge, foreshadowing the realization of another Dare County dream — the creation of a national memorial to the Wright brothers' first flight. Championed by W. O. Saunders, editor of the Elizabeth City *Independent*, this dream became a reality in 1931, when the cornerstone of the memorial was laid to commemorate the twenty-fifth anniversary of the first flight. In only 6 years, Dare County beaches had become accessible. Automobiles could now take the bridge across Currituck Sound, drive to Nags Head on a paved state road, and reach Manteo by crossing a bridge over Roanoke Sound and have the opportunity to stop at hotels, real estate developments, and a national aviation shrine along the way.

The Banks south of the Roanoke Island Bridge still had not changed much. The Depression was in full swing, adversely affecting the fishing economy, and two hurricanes in late 1933 damaged many houses and washed away most of the dunes that had protected them. The dunes attracted public attention first. By the spring of 1934, $1 million of public funds were made available to the Civilian Conservation Corps to begin building protective dunes along the beaches. Sand fences were strung along the berm to trap sand, and beach grasses were planted to hold the new palisade dunes in place. Later that spring, the North Carolina legislature took action to protect the grass by outlawing the practice of allowing livestock to range freely from Currituck to Hatteras Inlet. Local labor as well as transient workers were hired in the dune construction, so the loss of the poor grazing land was offset by the increase in employment opportunities—not a choice some wished to make, but at least some compensation.

Throughout the dune-building period, the idea of establishing a national park along the Outer Banks was slowly gathering support. This notion was first proposed by banker Frank Stick in 1933, but initial enthusiasm faded after the National Park Service took over operation of the Wright Brothers Memorial in 1933. In 1937 the park service recommended the establishment of the Cape Hatteras National Seashore Recreation Area. The proposed area centered on about 1,000 acres near Cape Hatteras Lighthouse that had been donated for public use by the Phipps, Guest, and Martin families. The park project was put on hold during World War II but was resuscitated by North Carolina congressmen thereafter. In 1952 private foundations managed by heirs of the Mellon family offered $618,000 for the purchase of park lands if the state would put up an equal sum. The state agreed within four days—surely an all-time speed record for state action. Thus, the creation of the Cape Hatteras National Seashore was assured. Following through on its commitments, the state then built an asphalt road from Nags Head to Ocracoke and established regular ferry service across the two inlets along the way.

The public infrastructure that allows human access to Banks environments was largely completed in the mid-1960s. Its existence has stimulated population and economic growth unparalleled in Banks history. Between 1970 and 1990, the Outer Banks population in Currituck and Dare counties tripled (from 13,971 to 36,482 full-time residents), seasonal housing more than tripled (from 1,919 to 7,512 units), and overnight lodging receipts almost quadrupled in the last decade alone (from $4.4 million to $16.9 million annually). It is hard to imagine how this growth can continue indefinitely. The issues facing the Banks' future seem to involve specific aspects of two general questions: how much development is enough, and what kind of public infrastructure should be put in place to support it? Natural scientists examining recent Banks history see limits to growth. Late nineteenth-century technology failed to sustain a Banks economy based on renewable living resources of fish and waterfowl. Can late twentieth-century technology sustain present levels of growth in an economy based on recreation and tourism? To examine that question, we will look first at fisheries, a Banks resource always susceptible to overexploitation and integral to recreational appeal, and then at water supply and wastewater disposal, two issues that will have an impact on future population levels.

Fisheries: A Resource at Risk from Overexploitation

Marine fisheries resources of North Carolina are diverse and productive but still susceptible to overexploitation. The commercial catch is comprised of 68 "types" of finfish and 15 species of shellfish. Some of the finfish types (groupers, hakes, jacks, snappers) are made up of several species each. The recreational catch contains 30 species, all but one of which (silver perch) is also caught commercially. The annual harvest of fish and shellfish has been recorded since 1880. It reached 210 million pounds in 1908, ranged upward to 300 million pounds in the late 1950s and 400 million pounds in the early 1980s, and sank below 200 million pounds in the mid-1970s and 1990s.

The reasons for the diversity of this fishery are related to habitat and geography. North Carolina is located at a point where ocean currents from the south (the Gulf Stream) and the north (the mid-Atlantic drift, a southern extension of the Labrador Current) meet and mix tropical and cold temperate zone animals in a warm temperate setting. The habitat range is equally broad: semitropical coral reefs near the Gulf Stream, warm temperate sand and coral bottoms on the continental shelf, and more than 2,500 square miles of inshore sounds and estuaries. All of these waters are productive — offshore, because of the Gulf Stream–influenced upwelling of high-nutrient waters; the continental shelf, because of up-welling and nutrient additions from the seafloor; and inshore, because nutrients from land runoff are trapped by tidal circulation (see Chapter 1).

The species that make up Banks fisheries use these habitats in three general ways: anadromous species (such as herring, shad, striped bass, and sturgeon) live most of their lives in the ocean but migrate into fresh-water to breed; estuarine migrators (such as menhaden, shrimp, flounder, and blue crab) spawn in the nearshore ocean but utilize estuaries and sounds as nursery areas for their larvae and juveniles; and resident species (such as clams and oysters) live in one general location without migrating extensively. The importance of inshore waters is shown by the fact that 90 percent of the commercial catch (by weight) and 60 percent of the recre-ational catch (by number) inhabit them during some part of their life cycle.

Despite any similarity in life cycles, each species has its own limit of sustainable harvest determined by the unique relationship between the number of spawners, spawning success, natural mortality, and fishing mortality. These factors control each species' abundance individually, but all species are influenced by variations in climate, water quality, and weather. As a result, data on total harvest may tell us something about the productivity of the habitat that supports fisheries but doesn't tell us much about the status of an individual species.

The status of fishery stocks is assessed one species at a time. Harvest rates don't tell us everything we need to know because the same size pop-ulation may be harvested heavily when the market price is high and light-ly when the price is low. As a result, fishery scientists sample adult pop-ulations independently of harvesters to estimate potential reproductive success. Data from the age and size composition of harvests, the amount of fishing effort, and fishery surveys are combined to produce mathemat-ical models of stock abundance and projections of future abundance. Such models are the best we can do, but they have proven notoriously fal-lible because of inadequate data, unexpected changes in migration pat-terns, and unpredictable weather.

The North Carolina Division of Marine Fisheries assembled available data to assess the stock status of the 30 most important fisheries species in 1992 in *Descriptions of North Carolina's Coastal Fishery Resources*. Its analysis shows 8 stocks (27 percent) to be healthy, 11 (37 percent) to be stressed, and 7 (23 percent) to be overfished. Four stocks (13 percent) can't be categorized with available data. Table 3 lists the species in each category and the reasons each is categorized as it is.

The characterizations in table 3 are the state's official assessment of stock status. They are based on the best information available to the agency responsible for making the assessments. However, it would probably be difficult to locate a single North Carolinian who would agree with all of the information in table 3. Disagreement is especially sharp between commercial and recreational fishers. These two groups have very different requirements, and expectations, concerning fishery stocks. Commercial fishers do not require dense or concentrated stocks because they can fish at the best possible time with the most efficient gear they can afford or devise. Commercial gear concentrates fish as it catches them. Sports fishers, on the other hand, can only do well when prey is densely concentrated and in areas accessible to their gear. The gear itself may be sporting but is certainly inefficient when compared to commercial gear. Sports fishers are further limited by the times they can fish — a bluefish blitz on a Tuesday morning is unlikely to generate fond memories for many surf casters, and an offshore school will generate none. A commercial fisher can exploit both situations and recognizes them as indications of fish abundance — a point lost on someone who sees neither phenomenon.

These differences account for much of the public argument and controversy between fishing groups. Sports fishers accuse commercial operators of ruining fishing by catching all the fish. Commercial fishers respond by claiming that there are plenty of fish but that some people just don't know when and where to find them. It sometimes seems that fishers can agree on only three things: that the official assessment of fishery stocks is wrong; that they, personally, have never done anything that could have reduced stocks; and that poor water quality created by people who live elsewhere has adversely affected coastal fishing. Those who hold these views are like the blind men who commented after examining different parts of an elephant, "All are partly in the right and also partly wrong." The truth is that different fish stocks are at different levels at dif-

Table 3. Status of Major Fish Stocks in 1992

	Basis for Classification

Healthy Stocks

Southern flounder	Satisfactory number of young; stable age class distribution
King mackerel	Low fishing mortality; many spawners
Spanish mackerel	Low fishing mortality; strong recruitment; increasing spawners
Atlantic menhaden	Low natural mortality; increasing spawners
Brown shrimp	Annual species; recent juvenile abundance and landings high
Pink shrimp	Annual species; recent juvenile abundance and landings high
White shrimp	Annual species; recent juvenile abundance and landings high
Blue crab	Recent juvenile abundance and landings high; decreasing catch per trap

Stressed Stocks

Spot	Reproduction adequate but adults fewer than expected and in 2-year classes only
Bluefish	Declining landings and catch per unit effort; fishing mortality increasing
Striped bass	Low landings; decreased range of age and size; reduced reproduction
American shad	Declining landings; poor water quality in critical habitat
Hickory shad	Sharp decline in recent landings; poor water quality in critical habitat
River herring	Recent declines in landings and catch per unit effort in pound nets; low juvenile abundance
Catfish	Decline in landings; poor water quality in critical habitat
Reef fish	Many species heavily overfished, others unknown; group is stressed
Hard clams	Declining harvests; heavy fishing pressure; poor water quality in critical habitat
Bay scallops	Decimated by algal bloom in 1987; heavy fishing pressure
Sharks	Some overfished, some not; group as a whole is stressed

Table 3. Continued

	Basis for Classification
Overfished Stocks	
Weakfish	Reduced landings and catch per unit effort; low numbers of mature fish; mediocre recruitment
Summer flounder	High fishing mortality; poor reproduction; decreased catches of mature fish
Atlantic croaker	Reduced landings, catch per unit effort, size, mature fish, and juvenile abundance
Red drum	High fishing mortality; low spawning stock and yield per recruit
Scup	Reduced landings, adult abundance, age range, and catch per unit effort; increased mortality rates
Black sea bass	Reduced catch per unit effort, adult abundance, and mature fish
Oyster	Stock and harvest declines; pollution, disease, and habitat degradation

Source: Data from North Carolina Division of Marine Fisheries, *Descriptions of North Carolina's Coastal Fishery Resources* (Morehead City: North Carolina Division of Marine Fisheries, 1992).

ferent times. Some stocks decline because of human activities (like over-fishing or pollution), but many wax and wane as a result of natural causes we do not fully understand.

The information summarized in table 3, although controversial in some details, reflects what is clear to most people: overfishing of many of North Carolina's diverse and productive fish stocks is occurring now. What is not clear is how to avoid making this situation worse without causing pain and controversy in the process. The pain and controversy result from the simple fact that all reduced fish stocks benefit from reduced fishing pressure. The pain of such reductions is made even worse because most gear—both sport and commercial—can catch several different species at the same time. Thus, attempts to reduce the catch of one overfished species often require reducing the use of gear that could catch other species. This is seen most strikingly in Albemarle Sound, where severe fishing restrictions on striped bass almost eliminated all commercial fishing. Pain will also result from the fact that some commercial fishers and gear types catch groups of species that are now stressed or overfished. Winter trawl fishing is an example. The predominant catch has historically been summer flounder and weakfish, now both heavily overfished. Secondary catches are black sea bass, croaker, and spot, the first two of which are overfished and the last, stressed.

Another problem is bycatch, or fish caught unintentionally while harvesting something else. Bycatch cannot be avoided altogether when nets are used; the very diversity and productivity that attract fishing in the first place result in multispecies catches. The problem of bycatch in shrimp fisheries has captured the most public attention. Shrimp stocks are healthy, but shrimp trawls can also catch sea turtles and finfish. Devices that prevent federally protected sea turtles from becoming trapped in nets are now required; devices to exclude finfish are being used voluntarily. Whether these devices work well enough to adequately protect non-target species from overfishing is questionable.

Controversy is the only sure outcome of attempts to diminish the overuse of natural resources. Controversy surrounds fishery regulations now and will sharpen as further efforts are made to reduce fishing so that stocks can increase. Much of the pain of this controversy is borne by commercial fishers. Victims of their own success, they have worked hard and intelligently to become efficient at what they do, but because they harvest a public resource, they are subject to public scrutiny. Some fishers feel they have been "demonized" by critics. In a sense, they are like the commercial hunters of the early 1900s; they have become efficient enough to overharvest the resources that support them. The trick is to recognize the early warning signs of resource overuse so as to avoid its full expression in resource decline and public controversy. Recognizing potential areas of resource overuse is technically difficult; acting on those signs to reduce the use of publicly held resources is even harder.

Recent experience with fisheries offers three important lessons for the future of the Outer Banks:

1. Natural resources cannot support infinite development.
2. Overuse of resources is difficult to recognize and avoid.
3. Controversy and human suffering occur when the adverse impact of overuse becomes obvious.

Outer Banks fisheries are not the only fisheries to demonstrate these lessons; unfortunately, ocean fisheries worldwide are in the same condition. One advantage of coastal fisheries is that the high reproductive capacity of most species (egg production in the tens of millions is not uncommon) suggests that better management may bring these populations back to former levels. North Carolina fisheries have bounced back twice during this century from harvest levels as low as those experienced now. Fishing restrictions on mackerel in Florida and striped bass in the mid-Atlantic states (including North Carolina) preceded dramatic increases in abundance. As in any exercise program, the rule of "no pain, no gain" applies and gives hope for the ultimate success of tomorrow's painfully restrictive regulations. Natural resources requiring recovery times longer than those of fecund coastal fish, however, will exact greater penalties on overuse. Freshwater supplies and wastewater disposal on the Banks are two examples.

Water Supplies: Rainfall, Groundwater, and Aquifers

Everyone on the Outer Banks drinks rainwater; the only difference between water supplies is in the amount of time the rainwater has been stored before being drunk. Life-saving station and lighthouse personnel drank rainwater relatively fresh. They collected rainfall by routing water directly from the roof into cisterns. These cisterns remain at many of the original late nineteenth-century structures on the Banks. Modern Bankers drink rain that has been stored longer before consumption. Most water supplied to Outer Bankers has been stored as groundwater — some for as little as a few weeks, some for longer than a decade — but all of it was rainfall not too long ago. Another source of even older rainwater lies 1,000 feet or more beneath the Banks, confined within a layer of limestone called the Castle Hayne formation. No one knows exactly how long ago the water in the Castle Hayne fell as rain on the coastal plain, but no one thinks it was very recently.

Two geological formations constitute the groundwater sources that provide all the freshwater used on the Outer Banks today: an upper aquifer that provides 5 million gallons per day to the northern Banks and up to 1.4 million gallons per day to the Cape Hatteras region and a deeper aquifer called the Yorktown formation that provides an additional 3 million gallons per day to Kill Devil Hills. Yorktown formation water is brackish and must be desalinated before it can be used. The Castle Hayne or limestone aquifer is a third potential source of freshwater for the Banks, but it, too, is brackish. All three of these aquifers, in addition to the "lower aquifer" beneath them, occur at or near the land surface inland from the Banks and become steadily deeper as they extend toward the sea. Figure 37 provides a map and hydrographic cross section of eastern North Carolina that illustrate the relationship of these features to one another.

The scale of figure 37 is too large to provide a real understanding of the upper aquifer as it occurs on the Outer Banks. This layer of freshwater exists in the spaces between grains of sand, which is included in hydrologists' definition of "rock." Saltwater occurs below and on the sides of the freshwater. The freshwater layer is called a perched water table because it is perched on top of a continuous layer of saltwater. Figure 38 illustrates this perching and the flow directions taken by rainfall that sinks into the freshwater lens from the top. The freshwater layer seems surprisingly deep until you realize that the freshwater is like an ice cube — its density is only slightly lower than the water around it, so it floats but displaces almost its own volume of the supporting liquid. Hydrological theory predicts that freshwater in a perched water table extends 40 feet deep for every foot that the water table extends above sea level. Unfortunately, this theory does not apply well to water tables along the Outer Banks. This is partly because freshwater mixes with the surrounding saltwater, so the full impact of the density difference between freshwater and seawater is not realized, and partly because layers of impervious silt and clay occur in some places (under Buxton Woods, for example), interfering with the free exchange of freshwater within the perched water table. As a result, the measured depth of the freshwater layer in Buxton Woods is only about 120 feet, despite a water table that is almost always more than 5 feet above sea level. Freshwater layers are rarely deeper than 30 feet in most of the narrow sections of the Outer Banks.

The shallowness of the freshwater layer under the Outer Banks has major implications for future water supplies. First, there just isn't very much freshwater stored between grains in the top 30 feet of sand. Productive wells from these sands may yield 25 to 100 gallons per minute for a while because the sand is porous and water flows readily toward the well (the good news), but since the freshwater is surrounded by saltwater, such wells are susceptible to contamination by saltwater drawn in from below or from the sides (the bad news). Second, the shallow freshwater layer moves up and down with the flowing and ebbing of ocean tides, thereby mixing water across the freshwater/saltwater boundary. Third, during storm tides, seawater may cover the top of the freshwater layer, creating brackish water at the top of the water table. Finally, and most unfortunately, prior use of the island sands for disposal of wastes — both human and industrial — has rendered shallow freshwater in some areas unfit for human consumption. This type of contamination necessitated extending a water supply pipe from Buxton to Avon to supplement local water supplies with water from beneath Buxton Woods.

The problems of maintaining freshwater supplies in narrow parts of the Outer Banks have focused increasing attention on the water supply potential of the wider parts, that is, at Cape Hatteras between Buxton and Frisco. The subsurface water situation in this area is somewhat different from that described above. The layer of freshwater extends quite deep (110 to 130 feet) and is separated from the saltwater below by a layer of clay and silt more than 50 feet thick. The volume of freshwater stored between sand grains above the clay layer is estimated to be about 33 billion gallons because the area available to store the water is large (about 10 square miles) as well as deep. Not surprisingly, this freshwater supply has not gone unnoticed during recent development of the Outer Banks. The Cape Hatteras Water Association (CHWA) was formed in 1965 to develop water supplies from this source. The association now has 44 wells reaching

Figure 37. Hydrologic areas and aquifers of eastern North Carolina. Note that the cross section showing the depth of aquifers illustrates the situation along transect A to A' on the inset map, from about Rocky Mount on Interstate 95 to the beach at Kill Devil Hills. Data from North Carolina Division of Water Resources Water Supply Studies and U.S. Geological Survey Hydrologic Investigations, summarized in M. D. Winner and R. W. Coble, *Hydrogeological Framework of the North Carolina Coastal Plain Aquifer System*, Open File Report 87-690 (Washington, D.C.: U.S. Geological Survey, 1989).

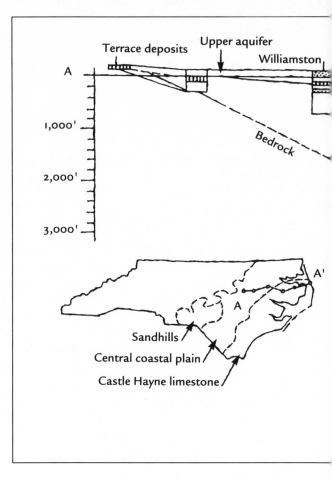

depths of 40 to 60 feet. Together, these wells can provide almost 1.4 million gallons of water per day, although to do so they must be pumped at more than double the rate of natural drainage in the vicinity of the wells. This is not considered a problem, however, because high pumping rates in the summer alternate with low pumping rates in the winter, when the aquifer is recharged with freshwater. Nevertheless, maximum pumping rates cannot be sustained for long periods, so much thought and growing

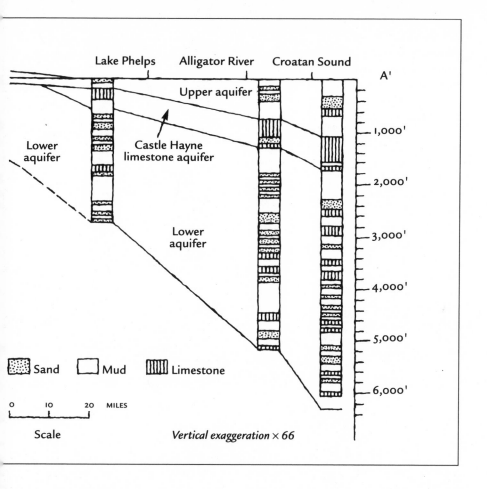

Lake Phelps Alligator River Croatan Sound

A'

Upper aquifer

Lower
aquifer

Castle Hayne
limestone aquifer

Lower
aquifer

1,000'

2,000'

3,000'

4,000'

5,000'

6,000'

Sand   Mud   Limestone

0   10   20   MILES

Scale   *Vertical exaggeration × 66*

controversy focus on the wisdom and/or the best method of extending the well field in the Hatteras aquifer.

Extending the area of the Hatteras aquifer or increasing the volume of water supplied from it raises issues involving almost every aspect of natural resource development. For starters, very different interests are involved at the local, state, and federal levels. Next, all the obvious conflicts exist between those hoping to see further development of the southern

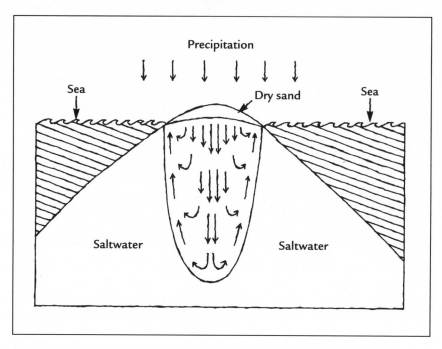

Figure 38. A "perched" water table under a barrier island. Arrows indicate the direction of water flow within the water table.

Banks and those hoping to preserve the few remaining natural areas. Finally, we have imperfect technical knowledge of the water resources being considered for development, a problem perhaps tied to all other issues.

Government and residents' interests differ. The CHWA, representing the local government, has applied for permits to extend the well field to meet the anticipated need for 4.5 million gallons per day by the year 2000 (more than triple the current maximum supply rates). The extension permit immediately brings state and federal governments into the picture because part of the extension would be located in sections of Buxton Woods owned by the state and designated an Area of Environmental Concern (AEC) in an effort to protect what remains of this undeveloped maritime forest. The extended well field would also be supplied by water draining from the Cape Hatteras National Seashore. The park service is concerned that such drainage would have a negative effect on aquatic areas of the national seashore. Those who hope to see greater private enterprise in Buxton and Hatteras favor the extension because they recognize that water supply is probably the single most important determinant of economic development. Environmentalists remain convinced that the AEC designation for Buxton Woods was wise, and many are willing to work to maintain that status. Much technical study of the Hatteras aquifer has been, is being, and will be carried out before this controversy is resolved. All participants agree that the Hatteras aquifer is a finite resource, but no one understands it well enough to settle differences of opinion concerning how much water can be supplied without causing an adverse environmental impact.

A technical understanding of the Hatteras aquifer system is not easy or cheap to attain. We do know some things about the aquifer, mostly from analyses of test wells and production wells drilled as part of the existing well field. This data provides the kind of information summarized in figure 39. Note that the freshwater table extends 5 to 10 feet above sea level, the confining bed of clay is at a depth of 120 feet, and the interface between fresh and saltwater along the southern border of the aquifer is irregular and varies with depth. The shape of the northern border of the aquifer is not known. We also know something about the areal extent of open water in swamps and ponds relative to the location of the current and proposed well fields (see figure 40). We are reasonably sure that present levels of residential development around the well field have not polluted the aquifer to any major extent because development is concentrated near NC 12 at the northern edge of the aquifer. We are equally confident that current pumping levels have not drawn seawater into the well field because chloride levels of pumped water have not increased during 20 years of pumping. We know that rainfall averages about 55 inches per year but has ranged from 90.8 inches (1989) to 41.5 inches (1965). It is estimated that the average annual rainfall provides enough water to completely fill the aquifer about every 12 years.

What we don't know about the aquifer is how changes in the water-removal rate will affect plant communities above it and saltwater en-

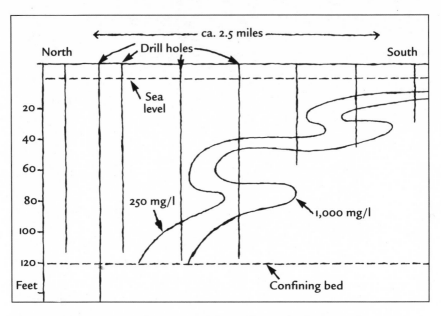

Figure 39. Cross section of Buxton Woods aquifer south of NC 12. Salt content of water is indicated by lines of equal chloride. Redrawn from Ralph C. Heath, "Ground-water Resources of the Cape Hatteras Area of North Carolina," report for the Cape Hatteras Water Association (1988), fig. 20, p. 54.

croachment into it. We need to know about these relationships if we hope to use the data to defuse controversy. We will also pay a high price for error because, unlike the potentially rapid recovery rates of coastal fish resources, maritime forests would take at least a century to recover if destroyed, and a saltwater-contaminated aquifer might never recover.

Unfortunately, hydrologists studying the Hatteras aquifer have quite different opinions about how to proceed in attempting to understand it. A National Park Service hydrologist has used available data to construct a mathematical model of groundwater flow. This model is based on admittedly inadequate data described as "preliminary," but it does provide some idea of how the aquifer might behave under different rainfall and water production regimes. The model predicts a maximum lowering of the

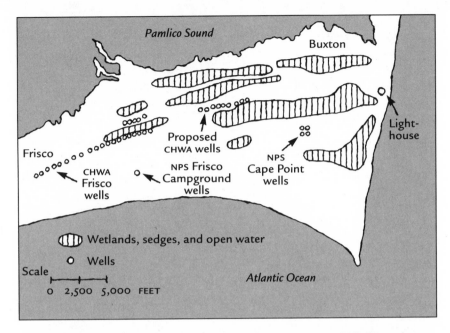

Figure 40. Freshwater ponds and wetlands near Cape Hatteras. This figure shows existing ponds and wetlands and existing and proposed well fields. Redrawn from Ralph C. Heath, "Ground-water Resources of the Cape Hatteras Area of North Carolina," report for the Cape Hatteras Water Association (1988), fig. 37, p. 106.

water table by 1.5 to 3 feet near the wells and by 1 foot over much of Buxton Woods if only 1.3 million gallons per day is withdrawn year-round. The park service is concerned by this prediction because this amount of lowering of the water table would certainly affect the Jeanette Sedge (the ponds west of Cape Hatteras Lighthouse) and the maritime forest throughout most of Buxton Woods.

Most hydrologists agree that much more information is needed before water table change or saltwater encroachment rates can be predicted with full confidence. Studies to provide the needed information have been undertaken by different agencies, including North Carolina State University and the North Carolina Department of Health, Environment, and Natural Resources. Additional data must be gathered on the distribution of sediment layers within the aquifer because it is not clear that water moves freely within the aquifer—an issue of significance for the encroachment of saltwater. We also need to know the rate at which water moves through the water-bearing strata and how much water can be stored within them. Current estimates of these measurements differ by factors of 2 to 4.

Wastewater Disposal: A Problem with No Good Solution

The freshwater supply may be the most important initial determinant of residential development, but inextricably linked to it are even more vexing problems of wastewater treatment and disposal. Water use per Banks resident is about 100 gallons a day, and 90 percent of that water is disposed of through drains and sewers. What happens next has major consequences for the Outer Banks environment and future development.

Most of the wastewater is treated and disposed of through privately owned septic tank systems. These systems typically consist of a precast concrete tank connected to a drain field made of perforated 4-inch pipe laid in trenches filled with crushed stone. The septic tank allows solid material to settle out of the wastewater, and the drain field disperses the wastewater over a broad area, where impurities are decomposed by bacteria and fungi in the soil. Septic tank solids must be pumped out periodically to prevent buildup and wastewater overflows, a service provided by private businesses.

Each septic tank system can effectively treat and dispose of wastewater generated by only a small number of people. Such systems work best for single-family dwellings but can be designed to serve small multifamily dwellings as well. Septic tank systems on the Outer Banks, however, are problematic. Many soil types are not suitable for drain fields, such as some on the Outer Banks, which are often too porous to allow time for wastewater impurities to decompose before entering the groundwater. This is especially true in areas of coarse sand. Fine sands make effective drain fields as long as the water table is not located too close to the surface, a requirement that cannot be met in low-lying areas of the Banks. Storms can also flood all Banks areas occasionally. The flooding of drainage trenches allows bacterial growth that clogs pipes, prevents the free passage of wastewater, and causes untreated sewage to escape and flow overland to nearby creeks or sounds.

Options other than septic tank systems must be utilized in many Outer Banks settings. The only other option now being used is a "package" system in which a small sewage collection network feeds wastewater into a central treatment and disposal system. Several facilities of this type now serve moderate-density developments (such as condominium complexes, residential developments, and hotels). The type of treatment and the method of wastewater disposal vary. Almost all plants have a settling chamber to remove solids and an area allowing some type of extended contact between wastewater and the bacteria that decompose organic material into plant nutrients like phosphorus and nitrogen as well as complex dissolved and particulate organic matter. Treatment is designed to destroy all human pathogens so that wastewater is not a health threat. The level of treatment and the method of disposal determine whether wastewater is an environmental threat.

Treatment plants can be designed to remove almost every contaminant from wastewater, but the more contaminants that are removed, the more expensive the operation becomes. As a result, most treatment systems leave some dissolved and particulate matter in the wastewater. Final decomposition takes place outside the plant and may use up the dissolved oxygen required by fish and shellfish in the receiving waters. Treatment plants can also be designed to remove phosphorus and nitrogen from wastewater but, again, only at considerable expense. Removal of nutrients is an issue because most coastal waters already have high concentrations of nutrients, and additional nutrients in wastewater can cause overgrowth of algae and algal "blooms," a heavy growth of algae that discolors natural waters, reduces their recreational appeal, and may kill fish. Additional plant nutrients certainly increase photosynthesis and plant growth rates in receiving waters. As a result, wastewater from treatment systems must be disposed of carefully to prevent adverse environmental impacts.

Five disposal options for treated wastewater exist: ocean discharge, sound discharge, land application, evaporation, and deep well injection. Only two of these options — sound discharge and land application — are currently used on the Outer Banks. Ocean discharge was considered in the mid-1980s but rejected; evaporation has not been used because it requires a great deal of fuel; and injecting wastewater into the ground is illegal in North Carolina.

Existing wastewater disposal systems disperse treated sewage onto the land or into the sounds. Dispersal on land may place wastewater onto the land surface or into the top layer of soil. To disperse wastewater onto the land surface, perforated pipes mounted onto two or more arms revolve around a central point, distributing wastewater onto the ground beneath. Such systems disperse 3 to 5 gallons per day per square foot, so highly porous soils such as dune sands are required for their proper operation. Subsurface dispersal systems work something like septic tank drain fields, in which perforated pipes are laid into trenches of crushed stone. Wastewater is delivered to such systems under low pressure so that the entire dispersal field is used simultaneously. Dispersal rates range from 10,000 to 50,000 gallons per day per acre (0.43 to 1.16 gallons per day per square foot), so less porous soils are suitable. Often these disposal fields are built above the land surface, appearing as low rectangular mounds. Wastewater dispersal into the sounds is accomplished through a pipe called an outfall that runs offshore and ends in a perforated section called a diffuser. Both ground and sound dispersal systems rely on the environment to accomplish the final stages of wastewater treatment. Dissolved organic matter is decomposed by bacteria and fungi, and nutrient chemicals are utilized by photosynthesizing plants or adsorbed and stored on the surface of sediment grains. In all cases, the potential exists for exceeding the capacity of the natural system to disperse or render harmless the material in the wastewater.

Septic tank and package systems for wastewater treatment and disposal can work well for low-to-moderate-density housing, but neither is foolproof and neither is appropriate for high-density populations. Septic tanks are best suited for treating wastes from individual homes. Package plant systems differ in size, but even the biggest ones can't handle a volume much larger than 100,000 gallons per day, the flow rate generated by about 1,000 people. Treating waste from more people will require central sewage collection and some type of municipal sewage treatment system. No such system exists on the Outer Banks today, the closest being at Skyco on Roanoke Island.

Existing Outer Banks sewage treatment systems seem to work surprisingly well. One of the most sensitive tests to identify ineffective systems is the presence of fecal bacteria in shellfish from waters into which treatment systems empty. Along the southern half of North Carolina's coast, such contamination is a large and growing problem and has resulted in the prohibition of shellfish harvesting by the Division of Shellfish Sanitation. Between Cedar Island (south of Ocracoke) and the South Carolina state line, the area closed to shellfish harvesting has grown from 37,000 acres in 1984 to 43,000 acres in 1994. North of Cedar Island to Virginia, the closed area has remained constant from 1979 to 1994 at about 6 percent of the total shellfishing area (about 9,000 acres). The closed areas are mostly small creeks that drain through residential regions serviced by septic systems.

Municipal sewage collection and treatment is so expensive and can have such a high capacity that large increases in residential population may be needed to pay for them. Municipal systems can differ in size, but the expense of sewage collection pipes and treatment facilities makes all of them larger than the systems utilized on the Banks today. Three relatively small municipal systems service the coastal communities of Carteret County, an area comparable to the Outer Banks located 60 miles to the south. The characteristics of Carteret County sewage systems are summarized in table 4.

All three Carteret County plants discharge wastewater into estuaries that drain into the sounds behind the barrier islands. Water quality in the receiving waters is affected, sometimes severely. The plants have been permitted to discharge wastewater with enough oxygen-consuming capacity to remove all the dissolved oxygen from a volume of natural water 4 to 5 times the discharge volume. The Morehead and Beaufort plants have been able to discharge an unlimited amount of ammonia, an important source of nitrogen in stimulating algal growth; the Newport plant has a limit of 7.5 to 15 milligrams per liter—5 to 10 times the concentration in

Table 4. Carteret County Municipal Sewage Systems in 1989

	Daily Treatment Volume	Miles of Collection Sewers	Pumping Stations
Morehead City	1.7 million gallons	35	12
Beaufort	1.5 million gallons	16	12
Newport	0.5 million gallons	12	4

Source: Data from North Carolina Division of Environmental Management, *Environmental Impact Statement: Carteret County Wastewater Treatment and Disposal* (Raleigh: North Carolina Department of Environment, Health, and Natural Resources, 1989).

the receiving waters. The plants have also been allowed to release fecal coliform bacteria in concentrations of 86 to 2,000 cells per 100 milliliters. The presence of fecal coliform bacteria in waters near clam and oyster beds has resulted in almost 3,000 acres of Carteret County shellfish waters being closed to shellfish harvesting between 1982 and 1992.

The full adverse environmental impact of municipal wastewater disposal may not be quite as bad as these numbers suggest, however, because some of the polluting materials settle rapidly and are incorporated into the bottom near the treatment plants. Some of the nitrogen also sinks to the bottom or rises into the air; not all of it stimulates plant growth in receiving waters. Many coliform bacteria may die after reaching the creeks, although some may live for considerable periods. Be that as it may, there is no question that the disposal of treated municipal sewage in coastal waters can and does have major adverse impacts. This fact is so widely accepted that it has been incorporated into National Coastal and Marine Policy, which seeks to "minimize the use of coastal and marine waters for wastewater disposal by strictly limiting ocean dumping, tightening controls on land-based sources, and establishing aggressive programs to reduce the amount of waste generated by our society."

The Outer Banks have grown to their current level of residential density without building large, publicly supported, central wastewater collection and treatment systems. They have thereby avoided much of the adverse environmental impact that such systems cause. For those considering the implications of building such a system, two examples are worth examining. Virginia Beach has a central system that disposes of wastewater through an ocean outfall. (A similar system costing $7.8 million was considered and rejected by Dare County in 1982.) Ocean outfalls currently cost about $2,000 per foot to build; Virginia Beach's outfall is 1.5 miles long with a mile-long diffuser extending further seaward. The Virginia Beach system has the capacity to dispose of 36 million gallons of sewage per day. Increased algal growth can be detected visually around the outfall, chlorophyll levels periodically rise to the highest level found acceptable, and concerns about the bacterial contamination of nearby beaches are omnipresent. South of the Banks, the cities of Wilmington and Wrightsville Beach in North Carolina also have central collection and treatment facilities. Wastewater from 14 million gallons of treated sewage per day is dumped into the Cape Fear River, which has the lowest level of water quality allowed by the state.

High-capacity centralized sewage disposal facilities can be characterized by three key traits: they are expensive; they can treat and dispose of volumes of domestic waste 10 to 100 times as large as can package plants; and they have adverse impacts on the environments into which they dump their wastes. The details differ depending on the specific size and type of centralized facility being considered, but all have these three characteristics. The secondary impacts of centralized facilities vary and are therefore hard to predict, but experience elsewhere (such as at Wrightsville Beach and Virginia Beach) suggests that alleviating waste disposal concerns by building a centralized system is followed by the rapid growth of residential construction and the demand for other types of public infrastructure and services. It is likely that, in the same way that road construction stimulated population growth on the Outer Banks in the early twentieth century and expansion of the water supply has stimulated population growth on the northern Banks today, construction of high-capacity wastewater treatment facilities will stimulate population growth in the future. It is almost certain that natural waters receiving wastewater from treatment plants will be environmentally degraded. Degradation has occurred wherever such systems have been built, although people may disagree about whether the level of degradation is acceptable. It is almost as certain that centralized waste disposal will increase the population and alter existing life-styles. Again, honest disagreements about the acceptability of such changes are possible.

Today's Bankers will decide what tomorrow's Banks will be like, just as yesterday's Bankers made decisions that resulted in today's unique mix of low-density development and preserved natural areas. The natural resources of the Banks are finite. We have seen what happens to fisheries when naturally sustainable harvest limits are exceeded. The human and economic disruption created by attempts to restore fishery resources to former levels has been painful. We know that roads and water supply have stimulated the growth of the human population on the Banks. Traffic and waste disposal problems are part of the result. Solving those problems will bring more population and new problems. "How much is enough?" is the main question for the future of the Outer Banks.

SUGGESTED READING

1. Environmental Processes

General Readings

Alexander, John, and James Lazell. *Ribbon of Sand: The Amazing Convergence of the Ocean and the Outer Banks*. Chapel Hill: Algonquin Books, 1992.

Bascom, Willard. *Waves and Beaches: The Dynamics of the Ocean Surface*. Rev. ed. New York: Doubleday, 1980.

Carter, R. W. G. *Coastal Environments: An Introduction to the Physical, Ecological, and Cultural Systems of Coastlines*. San Diego: Academic Press, 1988.

Leatherman, Stephen P. *Barrier Island Handbook*. Coastal Publications Series. College Park: University of Maryland Press, 1988.

Technical Readings

Godfrey, Paul G., and Melinda M. Godfrey. *Barrier Island Ecology of Cape Lookout National Seashore and Vicinity, North Carolina*. National Park Service Monograph Series. Washington, D.C.: Government Printing Office, 1976.

Stauble, D. K., and O. T. Magoon, eds. *Barrier Islands: Process and Management*. New York: American Society of Civil Engineers, 1989.

2. Guide to Field Sites: Corolla to Ocracoke

General Readings

Bishir, Catherine W. *The "Unpainted Aristocracy": The Beach Cottages of Old Nags Head*. Raleigh: North Carolina Department of Cultural Resources, Division of Archives and History, 1977.

Fussell, John O. *A Birder's Guide to Coastal North Carolina*. Chapel Hill: University of North Carolina Press, 1994.

Kraus, E. Jean Wilson. *A Guide to Ocean Dune Plants Common to North Carolina*. Chapel Hill: University of North Carolina Press, 1988.

Morris, Glenn. *North Carolina Beaches: A Guide to Coastal Access*. Chapel Hill: University of North Carolina Press, 1993.

Payne, Roger L. *Place Names of the Outer Banks*. Washington, N.C.: T. A. Williams, 1985.

Peterson, Roger Tory. *A Field Guide to the Birds East of the Rockies*. New York: Houghton Mifflin, 1980.

Pilkey, Orrin H., Jr., William J. Neal, and Orrin H. Pilkey, Sr. *From Currituck to Calabash: Living with North Carolina's Barrier Islands*. Research Triangle Park: North Carolina Science and Technology Research Center, 1978.

Stick, David. *Graveyard of the Atlantic: Shipwrecks of the North Carolina Coast*. Chapel Hill: University of North Carolina Press, 1952.

————. *North Carolina Lighthouses*. Raleigh: North Carolina Department of Cultural Resources, Division of Archives and History, 1980.

————. *The Outer Banks of North Carolina*. Chapel Hill: University of North Carolina Press, 1958.

Wilson, Elizabeth Jean. *A Guide to Salt Marsh Plants Common to North Carolina*. Raleigh: University of North Carolina Sea Grant, 1981.

Technical Readings

Inman, D. L., and R. Dolan. "The Outer Banks of North Carolina: Budget of Sediment and Inlet Dynamics along a Migrating Barrier Island System." *Journal of Coastal Research* 5, no. 2 (1989): 193–237.

Riggs, S. R., et al. "Depositional Patterns Resulting from High Frequency Quaternary Sea-Level Fluctuations in Northeastern North Carolina." *Society for Sedimentary Geology Special Publications* 48 (1992): 141–53.

3. Issues for the Future

General Readings

Ballance, Alton. *Ocracokers*. Chapel Hill: University of North Carolina Press, 1989.

DeBliev, Jan. *Hatteras Journal*. Golden, Colo.: Fulcrum Press, 1987.

Schoenbaum, Thomas J. *Islands, Capes, and Sounds: The North Carolina Coast*. Winston-Salem, N.C.: Blair Publishing, 1982.

Technical Readings

North Carolina Division of Environmental Management. *Environmental Impact Statement: Carteret County Wastewater Treatment and Disposal*. Raleigh: North Carolina Department of Environment, Health, and Natural Resources, 1989.

North Carolina Division of Marine Fisheries. *Descriptions of North Carolina's Coastal Fishery Resources*. Morehead City: North Carolina Division of Marine Fisheries, 1992.

North Carolina Division of Water Resources. *Currituck County Outer Banks Water Supply*. Raleigh: North Carolina Department of Environment, Health, and Natural Resources, 1991.

Winner, M. D., and R. W. Coble. *Hydrogeological Framework of the North Carolina Coastal Plain Aquifer System*. Open File Report 87-690. Washington, D.C.: U.S. Geological Survey, 1989.

INDEX

Agassiz, Louis, xi
Albemarle and Chesapeake Canal, 114
Albemarle Sound, 40, 52
Alligator River, 114
American beach grass (*Ammophila bre-viligulata*), 23, 50, 52, 88, 96, 99, 120
American Journal of Science, 4
American Revolution, 95
Anadromous species, 122
"Angle of repose," 48–49
Animal life, 96, 104
Aquifers, 128–35
Area of Environmental Concern (AEC) status, 132–33
Avon, N.C., 73, 112, 113, 129

Back Bay National Wildlife Refuge (Va.), 4, 60
Barlowe, Captain Arthur, 22, 41
Barrier islands, 1, 6–7; movement of, 6–7, 16, 22, 60, 94–95, 106; mainte-nance of, 21, 76; and rising sea level, 76, 95, 96. *See also* Outer Banks
Bass, 57, 59, 126, 127
Baum, Washington, 118–19
Beach accretion, 4, 10, 14, 15, 93
Beach cottages, 48, 55, 59, 73. *See also* "Unpainted aristocracy"
Beach erosion, 4, 6, 10, 14, 15, 21, 40–41, 49, 93–94; sound-side, 40–41; pace of, 49, 82; and residential construc-tion, 55, 59. *See also* Beaches; Erosion
Beaches, 93; migration of, 14–15; waves'

effects on, 89–91. *See also* Beach erosion
Beach grass. *See* American beach grass
Beaufort, N.C., 114, 139
Beech trees, 55
Bermuda wire grass, 49, 53
A Birder's Guide to Coastal North Caro-lina (Fussell), 64
Bird-watching, 57–58, 62, 64, 67, 70, 102, 103, 105. *See also* Waterfowl
Bishir, Catherine, 118
Bison, 59
Bitter tanic, 49, 53
Blackbeard's Camp, 96, 105
Black needlerush (*Juncus roemerianus*), 57, 70, 95, 104, 106
Black sea bass, 126
Blue crabs, 54
Bluefish, 41
Bodie Island, 62, 68, 69, 72
Bodie Island Dike Nature Trail, 62, 64, 66–67
Bodie Island Lighthouse, 62, 64, 66, 67, 112
Brackish water, 4, 88, 128, 129
Breakers: causes of, 9–11; collapsing, 10–11, 13, 14, 90; plunging, 10–11, 13–15, 90; spilling, 10–11, 14, 15, 90; and sand transport, 10–15, 106; sites to observe, 50, 90. *See also* Waves
Bridges, 66–69, 119
Buffalo, N.Y., 40
Buxton, N.C., 113, 129, 133

Buxton Woods, 29, 92, 128–29, 132–35
Buxton Woods Nature Trail, 80, 83–87, 91
Bycatch, 126

Caffey's Inlet, 57
California, 14
Canada geese, 62
Canadian Hole, 78; sites between Rodanthe and, 73–94
Canvasback ducks, 115
Cape Fear, 18
Cape Fear River, 141
Cape Hatteras, 66, 80, 81, 84–85, 96, 113; wind direction at, 9; difficulties of sailing around, 18, 109; freshwater at, 129–35. See also Cape Hatteras Lighthouse; Cape Hatteras National Seashore
Cape Hatteras Lighthouse, 80, 81, 92, 110, 112, 120, 135; erosion at, 2, 81–83, 110, 112; repairs to, 66; during Civil War, 74
Cape Hatteras National Seashore, 62, 64, 72, 120, 133
Cape Hatteras Water Association (CHWA), 129–30, 132
Cape Lookout, 18, 110
Cape Point, 43, 80, 87–92
Capes, 1, 18. See also names of specific Outer Banks capes
Carteret County, 139–40
Castle Hayne marl, 66, 128
Catbrier vine, 104
Cattails, 51, 57, 59, 70
Cedar Island, 139
Cedar trees, 27, 51

Chacandepeco Inlet, 80–81
Chesapeake Bay, 66
Chicamacomico Races, battle of (1862), 74, 88
Chickinacommock Inlet, 68, 72
Christmas trees: used to trap sand, 72
Cisterns, 74, 127
Civilian Conservation Corps, 73, 120
Civil War, 74, 88, 94, 108, 109–10, 118
Claptois, 90
Clarks, N.C., 113
Clark's Reef, 105
"Climax community," 104
Coastal currents, 90; and sand transport, 9, 16, 18, 20–22
Coastal Research Access Buggy (CRAB), 55
Coliform bacteria, 140
Colington Island, 54
Coots, 62
Coquina Beach, 62, 64–66
Corolla, N.C., 59, 97, 113; sites between Whalebone Junction and, 44–60. See also Corolla Lighthouse; Poyner Hill
Corolla Lighthouse, 44, 58–60. See also Currituck Beach Lighthouse
Cottonbush. See Groundsel
Crabs, 54, 104
Crab shedding, 54
Croakers, 41, 126
Currents. See Coastal currents; Tidal currents
Currituck Beach, N.C., 113
Currituck Beach Lighthouse, 112. See also Corolla Lighthouse
Currituck County, 120

Currituck Sound, 4, 57, 59, 115, 119
Cuspate forelands, 1

Dare County, 119, 120, 141
Deals, N.C., 113
Desalination, 128
Descriptions of North Carolina's Coastal Fishery Resources (North Carolina Division of Marine Fisheries), 123
Development: issues regarding, xi–xii, 55, 106, 107–42; north of Whalebone Junction, 44–49; on beaches, 48, 55, 59, 73; lack of planning in, 54, 58; planned, 55; and wildlife refuges, 58; economic, 108–21
Diamondback terrapins, 41, 118
Diamond City, N.C., 118
Diamond Shoals, 18, 81, 84, 90
Dolan, Robert, 6, 15
Drake, Sir Francis, 80
Drums (fish), 41
Duck, N.C., 44, 55–57
Ducks. *See* Waterfowl
Dune broom sedge (*Andropogon littoralis*), 26
Dune elder, 48
Dune grass, 72, 106
Dune ridges. *See* Sand ridges
Dunes: migrating, 4, 6, 7, 9, 22, 23, 25, 46–47, 106, 118; giant, 9, 48–49; "blown out," 23, 25; stabilization of by plants, 23, 25–26, 52, 53, 57, 72, 77; "cliffed," 23, 77, 100; plants found on, 23, 88, 99–100, 104; linear, 25; shape of, 25; "hummocky," 25, 52, 65; sites to observe, 48–49, 52, 57, 92–93; artificial, 64–65, 73, 76, 77, 96–97, 99,

120; rebuilt, 72, 96–97; palisade, 73, 76, 77, 96, 120; washing away of, 119–20. *See also* Sand; "Sand-sharing system"; *names of specific dunes*
Dune spurge (*Euphorbia polygonifolia*), 50, 88, 99

East Carolina University, 42
Ebb-tide deltas, 16, 19–20, 68, 69, 95
Eels, 41
Egrets, 62
Elizabeth City *Independent*, 119
Erosion, 4, 6, 10, 14, 40–41, 49, 68, 69, 94; sound-side, 40–41; pace of, 49; and residential construction, 55, 59; of dunes, 77, 100; resistance to, 80; efforts to prevent, 81–83. *See also* Beach erosion; Inlets: opening of; Sand: stabilization by plants
Estuarine migrators, 122
"Estuarine nursery areas," 42, 122

False Cape State Park (Va.), 60
Ferns, 51
Fiddler crabs, 104
A Field Guide to the Birds (Peterson), 64
Fire-wheel (*Gaillardia pulchella*), 50
Fishing, 42, 59, 88, 114–15, 119; rights, 115; commercial versus recreational, 123; gear, 125–26. *See also* Fish stocks
Fish stocks: as finite natural resource, xi, 108, 127; overharvesting of, 41, 115, 118, 121–27, 142; diversity of, 121–22. *See also* Fishing
Flagged trees and shrubs, 27, 73, 105
"Flats," the, 46, 48, 49, 66
Flooding. *See* Overwash events

Flood-tide deltas, 16, 19–20, 22, 57, 62, 68, 69, 80, 94–95, 106
Fort Fisher, 83
Freshwater: marshes, 4, 52, 57, 59, 62, 67, 70–71, 86, 92; lagoons, 4, 57, 62, 70, 83–84, 86, 92; creeks, 103. *See also* Water supply
Frisco, N.C., 16, 113
Frisco Campground, 80, 92–93
Frying Pan Shoals, 18
Fussell, John, 64, 70

Gallinules, 62
Gars, 41
Geese, 62. *See also* Waterfowl
Golden aster (*Heterotheca subaxillaris*), 50
Goldenrods, 51
Grasslands. *See* Prairies
Graveyard of the Atlantic (Stick), 50, 112
Greenbrier vine, 104
Groins, 81–82
Groundsel (cottonbush) (*Baccharis halimifolia*), 26, 48, 88, 92, 98, 103
Groundwater, 127–35
Guest family, 120
A Guide to Ocean Dune Plants Common to North Carolina (Kraus), 50
Gulls, 62, 70
Gum trees, 51
Gunt Inlet, 62, 68

Hammock Hills Nature Trail, 29, 96, 102–5
Hammocks, 71, 105
Hang-gliding, 1, 53
Harpers New Monthly Magazine, 118

Hatteras aquifer, 129–35
Hatteras Inlet, 4, 68, 93, 94–95, 114
Hatteras Island, 80–94, 109. *See also* Hatteras Village
Hatteras/Ocracoke ferry, 93, 94–95
Hatteras Pines, 80, 91–92
Hatteras Village, 80, 93–94, 118, 133
Hattorask Inlet, 62, 68
Hawaii, 14
Herbert C. Bonner Bridge, 66–69
Herons, 62
Herring, 115
Highway construction, 119, 120, 142
Holly trees, 51, 55
Horses, 59, 97–98
Horseweed, 99
Hunting, 62, 64, 70, 115, 118, 121
Huron shipwreck, 50, 112
Hurricanes, 4, 66, 68, 81, 83, 86, 92–93, 97, 119. *See also* Storms

Ibis, 62
Ice ages, 6–7, 29
Indus River, 20
Infrastructure investment, 108–15, 119–21, 139–42
Inlets: number of current and former, 2; sand deposition in, 4, 6, 16, 18, 23, 69, 80; opening of, 4, 40, 80, 94; closing of, 4, 57, 80; dynamism of, 16, 19–22, 62, 67, 68–71, 80–81, 93, 94; "throats" of, 19; bypass system, 20–22; stabilization of, 21–22; observation of processes in, 68. *See also names of specific inlets*
Inman, Douglas, 6, 15
Intracoastal Waterway, 114

National Academy of Sciences, 110
National Audubon Society, 57–58
National Coastal and Marine Policy, 140
National Park Service, 73; policies on protection of construction, xii, 66; plantings by, 53, 67; and Ocracoke Island, 95–96; and dune restoration, 97; and Wright Brothers National Memorial, 120; and freshwater supply, 133–35. *See also* Buxton Woods Nature Trail; Salvo Campground
Native American Museum, 92
Native Americans, 41, 92
Natural resources: finite nature of, xi, 107, 127, 142; renewable, 121
Nature Conservancy, 51
Nature trails, 51, 57, 62, 64, 70, 83–87, 102–5
Navigation: channels, 4, 21, 68, 94, 95; landmarks used in, 9, 81; difficulty of along Outer Banks, 16, 18–20, 109
NC 12 (highway), 43, 48, 49, 51, 55, 62, 73, 100, 102, 105; and storm damage, 2, 71–72, 96, 97; repairs to, 66, 72, 97
NC 12 Task Force, 97
New Buxton Inlet, 80–81
New Currituck Inlet, 57
New Inlet, 68, 71–72
Newport sewage treatment plant, 139
Nile River, 20
Nixon, Francis, 44
North Carolina Coastal Area Management regulations, 82
North Carolina Department of Health, Environment, and Natural Resources, 135

North Carolina Department of Transportation, 72, 81, 97
North Carolina Division of Marine Fisheries, 122–23
North Carolina Division of Shellfish Sanitation, 139
North Carolina legislature, 120
North Carolina Office of Coastal Management, 97
North Carolina State University, 72, 135
Nutrients: in sounds, 41–42; in ocean, 121–22; in wastewater, 137

Oak trees, 51, 55, 59, 86. *See also* Live oak trees
Ocean Bay Boulevard, 44, 50–51
Ocracoke Inlet, 4, 94, 95, 114
Ocracoke Island, 95–105; maritime forest on, 29, 38; Pony Pen on, 96, 97–98. *See also* Hatteras/Ocracoke ferry; Ocracoke Village
Ocracoke Village, 118
Offshore islands. *See* Barrier islands
Offshore sandbars, 15–16, 50. *See also* Offshore shoals; Sandbars
Offshore shoals, 16, 18. *See also* Sandbars
Old Hatteras Inlet, 94
Oregon Inlet, 62, 68–70; opening of, 4, 66, 68; sand deposition in, 16, 67–69; lighthouse at, 66; attempts to stabilize, 2, 69–70. *See also* Herbert C. Bonner Bridge
Outer Banks: environmental processes on, xi, 1–42, 106; development issues on, xi–xii, 55, 106, 107–42; unique

features of, 1, 6, 80; temperature on, 1, 40; as "Graveyard of the Atlantic," 18, 112; visitors to, 44; narrow sections of, 57, 93, 95; wide sections of, 62, 80, 84–85, 95; during Civil War, 74, 88, 94, 109–10, 118; economic development of, 108–21; population of, 109, 120, 142; employment on, 112–13, 119–20. *See also names of specific sites*

The Outer Banks of North Carolina (Stick), 109, 112, 114

Outfall pipes, 138, 141

Overgrazing, 22–23, 97–98, 118, 120

Overharvesting of fish stocks, 41, 115, 118, 121–27, 142

Overwash deposits (fans), 16, 76, 96

Overwash events, 6, 22, 40, 106; and sand transport, 16, 23, 65, 76, 93, 106, 119–20; sites showing evidence of, 49, 65, 71–72, 74, 76, 96–98; repair of damage from, 66, 72, 96, 97; ignoring of, 73; environmentally insensitive response to, 97; and sewage problems, 137

Oysters, 115

Package systems, wastewater treatment, 137, 138–39, 141

Palisade dunes, 73, 76, 77, 96, 120

Pamlico Sound, 40, 52, 74, 114

Parker's Creek, 96, 98–100

Pea Island National Wildlife Refuge, 62, 69, 70–72

Pelicans, 62

Pennywort (*Hydrocotyle bonariensis*), 50, 99

Pepper vine, 104

"Perched" water table, 92, 103, 128–29

Peterson, Roger Tory, 64

Phipps family, 120

Pine Island Audubon Sanctuary, 57–58

Pines, 51, 57, 73, 86, 96, 105; loblolly, 28, 51, 67; slash, 28, 66, 103–4; forests of, 51, 104

Plants: and sand stabilization, xi, 22–39, 49, 50, 52, 53, 57, 67, 72, 77, 96, 106; animals' overgrazing of, 22–23; range of, 23; salt spray effects on, 25–28, 51–52, 73, 74, 100, 104, 105; on dunes, 50, 88; in Nags Head Woods, 51–52; in marshes, 57; endangered, 70; and overwashes, 96. *See also names of specific plants*

Plovers, 70, 88

Pollution, 42, 129, 139–42. *See also* Wastewater disposal

Ponies, 59, 97–98

Pool, W. G., 47–48

Porpoises, 41

Port Lane Inlet, 62, 68

Portsmouth, N.C., 118

Poyner Hill, 49

Prairies, 23, 25, 66

Prickly pear cactus, 99, 104

Pungo River, 114

Punt guns, 115

Rabbits, 104

Raccoons, 104

Raleigh, Sir Walter, 62, 80

Rays, 41

Reagan, Ronald, 58

Red cedar (*Juniperus virginiana*), 26, 103

Seasonal cycles, 6
Sea turtles, 41, 72, 118, 126
Septic tanks, 65, 136–38
Sewage, 136–42. *See also* Wastewater
 disposal
Shad, 115
Shearwaters, 62
Shellfish, 139, 140
Shipbuilding, 118
Shipwrecks, 74; causes of, 18; remains
 of, 49–50, 64–65, 76, 99; museums
 on, 74; Spanish, 97; numbers of, 112
Shoals. *See* Offshore shoals
Shoreface recession. *See* Landward
 retreat
Shrimp, 126
Shrublands. *See* Thickets
Slash pines, 28, 66, 103–4
Smooth cordgrass (*Spartina alter-
 niflora*), 57, 70, 95, 105
Snow, 40
Snow geese, 62
Soft-shelled crabs, 54
Soil: organic matter in, 25, 28, 38;
 addition to dunes, 53; Castle Hayne
 marl, 66, 128; Yorktown formation,
 128
Sounds, 40–42. *See also names of specific
 sounds*
Soundside Road, 44, 46–50, 118
South Beach, 92
Southern bayberry. *See* Wax myrtle
Southern Shore Woods, 55
Spaniards, 59, 97
Spanish bayonets, 99, 103, 104
Spots (fish), 126
Squareback crabs, 104

Stick, David, 50, 109, 112, 114
Stick, Frank, 120
Storms, 1–2, 9, 80; and sand-sharing
 system, 15–16; and overwash events,
 16, 40, 49, 65, 72. *See also* Hurricanes
Storm surges, 9
Striped bass, 127
Sturgeon, 41, 118
Summer flounder, 126
Swales. *See* Ridge and swale topog-
 raphy
Swamp rose (*Rosa palustris*), 59

Tate, Will, 113–14
Teach, Edward (Blackbeard), 105
Temperature, 1, 40
Terns, 62, 70, 88
Terrapins, 41, 118
Thickets, 25, 26–28, 48, 52, 57, 58, 62,
 66, 67, 93, 95, 96, 101, 102–3, 105, 106;
 canopies of, 27–28; wedged, 28, 73,
 98–99; shrubs in, 49, 103; flagged
 plants in, 73, 105; range of plants in,
 88, 92, 103, 104
Tidal currents, 18, 19, 68, 69, 94
Tidal deltas, 20, 68. *See also* Ebb-tide
 deltas; Flood-tide deltas
Tidepools, 15
Tides, 9, 16, 19, 68. *See also* Ebb-tide
 deltas; Flood-tide deltas; Tidal cur-
 rents; Tidepools
Tourism, 118–21
Trade, 109–10
Trees: flagged, 27; Christmas, 72. *See
 also names of specific trees*
Trent, N.C., 113
Trout, 41

Tsunamis, 9
Tundra swans, 62

University of Kentucky, 59
"Unpainted aristocracy," 46–49, 118
The "Unpainted Aristocracy": The Beach Cottages of Old Nags Head (Bishir), 118
U.S. Army Corps of Engineers, 69, 96
U.S. Army Corps of Engineers Coastal Engineering Research Center, 44, 55–57
U.S. Coast Guard, 112
U.S. Congress, 51, 110, 115
U.S. Fish and Wildlife Service, 70, 72, 88
U.S. Life-Saving Service stations, 59, 73–74, 76–77, 108, 109, 112
U.S. Light House Board, 110
US 158 (highway), 43, 48, 49, 51, 55, 62
U.S. Postal Service, 113–14
US 64 (highway), 43
US 264 (highway), 43
U.S. Weather Service, 9, 112–13

Vegetation. *See* Plants
Virginia Beach, Va., 141
Virginia creeper, 104
Virginia Dare Trail, 48–51, 54–55

Wash Woods, N.C., 113
Wastewater disposal: as development issue, xi, 108, 121, 136–42; and nutrients, 42, 137. *See also* Pollution
Water: sand transport by, 9–22; tidal exchanges of in inlets, 19; and impact of sounds, 40. *See also* Brackish water; Freshwater; Marshes; Pollu-
tion; Saltwater; Water supply; Water table; Waves
Water Association Road, 80, 91–92
Waterfowl, 57, 62, 70, 105; hunting of, 115, 121. *See also* Bird-watching
Water oaks (*Quercus nigra*), 59
Water supply: as development issue, xi, 105, 121, 127–36, 141, 142; and plant life, 25; amount used, 136. *See also* Brackish water; Pollution; Water table
Water table, 92, 103, 128–29
Watt, James, 58
Wave base, 15
Wave climate, 55
Waves, N.C., 73, 112
Waves: causes of, 9; and sand transport, 9–22, 106; sites to observe, 50, 89–90; records of, 55, 57; erosion by, 77, 100; interactions between, 90; interactions between seafloor and, 9, 90–91. *See also* Breakers
Wax myrtle (southern bayberry) (*Myrica cerifera*), 48, 88, 92, 98, 99, 103
Weakfish, 126
Wechter, Nell Wise, 112
Wedged thickets, 28, 73, 98–99
Weiland, G. R., 4
Well capacity, 129, 130
Wetlands, 57, 86, 92. *See also* Marshes
Whalebone Junction, N.C., 43; sites between Corolla and, 44–60; sites between Rodanthe and, 60–73
Whales, 41, 118
Whales Head, N.C., 113
Whaling, 118
White, John, 41

Wildlife refuges, 58, 60, 62, 70–72, 92
Willow trees, 51
Wilmington, N.C., 141
Winds, 1, 53, 78; direction of, 7, 9, 15, 49, 52; sand transport by, 7–9, 49, 66, 106; and shipwrecks, 18; and stabilization of sand by plants, 23; speed of, 25, 26; sculpting of trees by, 74, 105. *See also* Salt spray exposure
Windsurfing, 78
Wright, Orville, 53–54, 114
Wright, Wilbur, 53–54, 113–14

Wright Brothers Memorial Bridge, 119
Wright Brothers National Memorial, 51, 53–54, 119, 120
Wrightsville Beach, 141
Würm glaciation, 29

Yaupon holly (*Ilex vomitoria*), 26, 48, 77, 88, 92, 98, 103
Yorktown formation, 128

Zonation patterns, 70–71, 95, 104, 105